Never Let A Ginger SNAP!

Life As A Redhead
Imparting Knowledge
Dispelling Myths

Claudia Hagen

This book may not be reproduced in whole or part without written permission from the author.

All rights reserved.
Copyright 2020 by Claudia Hagen
Published: September 2020 by
CreateSpace Independent Publishing Platform.

ISBN: 9798684510014

All quoted material and research obtained from interviews, reports, documents, news stories, magazine articles, websites, social media sites, and/or books listed in the Bibliography.

All photographs, unless otherwise credited, obtained from accessing public archives or from the personal property of the author.

Front and back covers designed and created by
Marty Bicek, Bicek Photography
Modesto, California.
Copyright 2020

For Brady, & Morgan -
thanks for the idea!

Ruadh gu brath - Redheads Forever

Table of Contents

Dedication   - - - - - - - -   3

Introduction   - - - - - - - -   6

Sonnet to Red-Haired Girls - - - - - -   11

Ode to Redheads   - - - - - - - - -   12

1. Realization of the Curse - - - - -   15

2. My Redheaded Superheroes - - - 26

3. I Am A Mutant Anomaly-Really - 39

4. The Red Inheritance - - - - - - -   52

5. Hairy History Horrors - - - - - - - 60

6. Paranormal Superpowers - - - - - 69

7. The Golden Crown - - - - - - - -   81

8. Sun Dots   - - - - - - - -   91

9. Rare & Radiant   - - - - - - - -   99

10. Medical Mysteries & Marvels - - 112

11. Fiery & Fiesty   - - - - - - - - - 132

12. Fire & Ice   - - - - - - - - 149

13. Redhead Potpourri - - - - - - - - 166

    Redhead's Yellow Teeth - - - - - 166

    Redhead's Sense of Scents - - - 169

    Redheads vs Insects - - - - - - - 173

14. Redhead Oddities - - - - - - - - - 183

    Metal Sensitivity - - - - - - - - - 183

    Static Shocks   - - - - - - - - - - 185

Table of Contents
(continued)

Endometriosis - - - - - - - - - - 189

Industrial Deafness - - - - - - - 194

15. South Park Gingervitis - - - - - - - 200

16. International Redhead Days - - - 206

Afterword - - - - - - - - - 211

Acknowledgements - - - - - - - - - 214

Bibliography - - - - - - - - - 217

Introduction

I was born with a thick mop of dark rusty red hair which has now aged to snow white. No, I don't have seven dwarfs following me around singing the "Heigh-Ho, Heigh-Ho," song - darnit. I have at least a bazillion freckles which have faded a bit with age. People might think they are old age liver spots, but just a few minutes in the sun will pop them back to full freckle flashing status.

Growing up in the 1950s there were very few redheads, at least it seemed that way to me. We were social outcasts, weirdos, devils, carrot tops, rusty, coppertops, copperheads, Duracells, pumpkin heads, reds, Commies, redfros, and some names not print worthy for a family centered book. I was not called, nor had I ever heard the term "Ginger" until I had grandchildren who were blessed with the curse - I mean, they were born with red hair. Ginger was, and still is, a common descriptive of redheads in the United Kingdom and Northern European countries. Eventually, the term made its way across the great Atlantic pond to America. In Australia, redheads are known as rangas (from the same color hair as orangutans) or blueys (the mid-1800s slang for fighters).

Introduction

Although most redheads are more of an orange color, there was no recorded word for "orange" until the late 1400s. The term 'redhead' has actually been used in recorded history since 1510. In this book, I will interchangeably use the two terms reds and gingers in describing redheads.

Today, we see redheads everywhere! They have a range of different red colors, from strawberry blondes to deep reddish auburns. They appear in print advertising, movies, television sitcoms, commercials, school yards, or as your elderly neighbor lady three doors down. In 1953, Disney introduced redheaded Peter Pan as *The Boy Who Wouldn't Grow Up*. Currently, Disney's redheads include Ariel (*The Little Mermaid*), Merida (*Brave*), Anna and Hans (*Frozen*) as well as several human redheaded characters; Amy Adams comes to mind first.

A short list of true redheaded actresses and celebrities include: Julianne Moore, Marcia Cross, Marg Helgenberger, Naomi and Wynonna Judd, Susan Sarandon, Nicole Kidman, Sissy Spacek and her daughter Schuyler Fisk, Carol Burnett, and Shirley Maclaine. Marilyn Monroe was a natural redhead but dyed her hair platinum blonde.

Introduction

Of course, some Hollywood reds are not true redheads but bottle borne. You may be surprised then disappointed to learn the following are bottle reds: Rita Hayworth (born with black hair), Lucille Ball (born brunette), Debra Messing (born with brown hair), Gillian Anderson (born dark blonde), Julia Roberts (born blonde)... the list is long for the fake red females.

Are there male actors and celebrities with true red hair? Yes! More and more everyday. Here is a short list: James Cagney, Ewan McGregor, David Caruso, Rupert Grint, Prince Harry, Mark McGuire, Boris Becker, Mario Batali, Scott Thompson aka Carrot Top, Shaun White, Ed Sheeran, Dale Earnhardt, Jr., and more.

A 2014 "Upstream Analysis" report found thirty percent of television commercials during primetime featured one or more redheaded characters, real, non-human, or animated: Wendy's hamburgers and Ronald McDonald both come to mind first (food!); Sprint, Verizon, Consumer Cellular, Kia, Skittles candy, Coca Cola, Dominoes Pizza, and many other familiar brands. All these advertisements feature a redhead, usually an attractive female, in a fifteen, thirty, or sixty second commercial spot. I challenge you to start

Introduction

watching for redheads (male, female, cute children, or even animated characters) appearing in television commercials. You will be amazed at the number you see.

Redheads have appeared in magazine advertisements long before television went colorized. They have always been an advertiser's dream come true. Why? Because redheads are memorable, attractive, rare, and unique. They make the reader or viewer (especially in ads targeting men) pay attention and remember the product advertised.

Have I peaked your interest in learning about the novelty of redheads? We are rare, attractive, attention getters, we can be comical, temperamental, possess super powers not well known, we are medically mysterious, and we are all definitely memorable - even though we all may not appear in advertisements.

The purpose in writing this book is to educate, amuse, explore facts, and dispel myths about redheads. I will present this by guiding readers through my redheaded history from realization of the curse forward; the trials, tribulations, and triumphs. All with humor along the way!

Introduction

New words for your vocabulary are <u>underlined</u> for emphasis and your own research, if so inclined.

Each chapter will feature quips I have come across in my research from a variety of sources, or made-up on my own. I call them *redheadisms*.

I am not a scientist, nor physician. I am a redhead first, a retired registered nurse (41 years in the trenches) second, and a mom, grandma, and great-grandma as well. I have researched the medical and scientific information presented here to the best of my ability and understanding. Collective interviews were done <u>uns</u>cientifically and anonymously via several redhead member social media sites (listed in the Bibliography).

I am so sorry the pictures throughout the book could not be in color. Many are old and not up to print quality in todays techno world.

Forge on oh great reader, through the thick forest of living redheaded. But BEWARE! You can never fully understand a redhead, nor should you ever try. Hopefully, this book will assist you in some small way. In any case, you will never be the same having known one!

A redhead is like a four leaf clover:
hard to find and lucky to have.

Redheads never suffer from a lack of attention.

Sonnet to Red-Haired Girls

Ye red-haired girls who in this world do dwell
Among the black-haired beauties all around,
List ye, while in my kindred heart doth swell
A love and consolation to abound
To all my fellow sufferers combined—
They call us "Freckles," "Carrot-top" and such;
But do not weep, perhaps they're beauty blind—
Have not great painters dared attempt as much
As beauteous women, all with Titian hair?
So laugh and sing, and held your temper, too,
And cease, my friends, that earnest, hopeful pray'r
That those bright locks take on a darker hue,
Forget the taunt a thoughtless comrade hurls,
A crown of glory's thine, oh, red-haired girls!

Augusta Roberts, 1925

Written by the presumably red haired Senior, Augusta Roberts, in her 1925 Decatur High School yearbook, Decatur, Georgia.

Ode To Redheads

Red hair is a woman's game.
The harsh truth is, most red-haired men look like blondes who've spoiled from lack of refrigeration. They look like brown-haired men who've been composted. Yet that same pigmentation that on a man can resemble leaf mold or junk yard rust, a woman wears like a tiara of rubies.

Not only are female redheads frequently lovely but theirs is a loveliness that suggests both lust and danger, pleasure and violence, and is, therefore, to the male of the species virtually irresistible. Red-Code-Red were the tresses of the original femme fatale.

Of course, much of the "fatale" associated with redheads is illusory, a stereotypical projection on the part of sexually neurotic men. Plenty of redheads are as demure as rosebuds and as sweet as strawberry pie. However, the mere fact that they are perceived to be stormy, if not malicious, grants them a certain license and a certain power. It's as if bitchiness is their birthright. By virtue of their coloration, they possess an innate permit to be terrible and lascivious, which, even if never exercised, sets them apart from the

Ode To Redheads

remainder of womankind, who have traditionally been expected to be mild and pure.

Now that women are demolishing those old misogynistic expectations, will redheads lose their special magic, will Pippi Longstocking come to be regarded as just one of the girls? Hardly. To believe that blondes and brunettes are simply redheads in repressive drag is to believe that UFOs are kiddie balloons. All redheads, you see, are mutants.

Whether they spring from genes disarranged by earthly forces or "planted" here by overlords from outer space is a matter for scholarly debate. It's enough for us to recognize that redheads are abnormal beings, bioelectrically connected to realms of strange power, rage, risk, and ecstasy.

What is your mission among us, you daughters of ancient Henna, you agents of the harvest moon? Are those star maps that your freckles replicate? How do you explain the fact that you live longer than the average human? Where did you get such sensitive skin? And why are your curls the same shade as heartbreak?

Ode To Redheads

Alas, inquiry is futile: Either they don't know or they won't say - and who has the nerve to pressure a redhead? We may never learn their origin or meaning, but it probably doesn't matter. We will go on leaping out of our frying pans into their fire, grateful for the opportunity to be titillated by their vengeful fury, real or imagined, and to occasionally test our erotic mettle in the legendary inferno of their passion.

Redheaded women! Those blood oranges! Those cherry bombs! Those celestial shrews and queens of copper! May they never cease to stain our white-bread lives with super-natural catsup.

Written by author Tom Robbins. Published in *GQ Magazine,* June 1988.

Chapter 1

Realization Of The Curse

I was a redhead before it was cool.
I became aware that I am rare.

The sky was a deep blue with big puffy white clouds that eventful day. The air was sweet with the scent of lilacs and other springtime flowers. My brand new forest green J.C. Higgins bike sparkled in the sunlight. A week or so earlier, Dad took me downtown to the big Sears store and bought this two-wheeled rolling piece of freedom for my sixth birthday. After the purchase we went to a nice restaurant for a father-daughter lunch. While I was enjoying my cheeseburger, fries, and chocolate milkshake, he explained the rules of the bicycle road and the parental house rules for riding. As he yammered on about staying on the right side of the road, no riding after dark, no hands-free riding… I nodded at the appropriate times, chewed and slurped while I envisioned myself riding on the yellow center line with my hands high in the air, wind in my hair, peddling furiously down the street to visit my friend Susan.

I had personally wiped down J.C. (my bike's name) with Windex and an old cloth diaper. She looked marvelous! We were ready to hit the road. Although my friend Susan lived just two country blocks from our house, it was the thought of getting away from my younger sister and two little brothers that made my bike rides so enjoyable. FREEDOM! I hopped on and ventured out, careful to stay on the right side of the road until I was out of view of mother's watchful eyes. I waved at the neighbor lady picking her prized roses then veered to the center yellow line.

The author on her beloved J.C. ready to roll.

I would amuse myself when riding by reasoning that staying in the center of the center line was a test of my biker balance skills. They were excellent of course, until I lifted my hands in the air. J.C. would get a little wobbly on me so I had to quickly grab the handlebars to resume perfect control. Hands-free riding was a work in progress. More practice was all I needed.

There was a two story brick house three doors down from our house and across the street from Susan's. An obnoxious boy lived there, about the same age as me, who was never seen outside playing. Instead, he would step out on his back porch and give the stink eye to any kid passing by.

On this particularly beautiful day with the breeze ruffling my long red hair, J.C.'s front wheels rolling exactly in the center of the center line, I raised my arms up (practicing for perfection) just as the obnoxious one stepped out onto his porch and yelled, "HEY!"

Scared the crap right out of me. Lost control of J.C. and crashed into the huge blooming lilac bush on the side of the road. The obnoxious one - we'll call him Carl - was doubled over laughing and pointing at me as I recovered myself and J.C. from the dense fragrant bush. I rode on to Susan's house without further incident, both hands on the handlebars, scraped arms, skinned knees smarting, and a very bruised ego.

Fast forward to a few days later, Carl evidently figured out my riding schedule. He was always waiting on the porch to yell at me. "HEY CARROT TOP! Keep your hands on the handlebars," or "HEY CARROT TOP, you need training wheels?" or any other stupid six year old remark followed by fits of laughter. If I ignored him, he would throw little pebbles at me or yell louder, but he always stayed on that little porch.

He was starting to piss me off and I had a short fuse at that age. I wanted to knock him senseless.

I asked my mom why he keeps calling me carrot top. She said it was because of my red hair, "Get used to it," she said. "Well that's just stupid. That kid is stupid," was my all-knowing reply. Carrots have green tops, not red I reasoned to myself. Well, I guess he could have called me carrot-butt instead or pumpkin head, so I'll stop complaining. That day, Mom and I had a lengthy discussion concerning the trials and tribulations of having red hair. She had rusty red hair as a kid until it turned more auburn in her teens. My sister and brothers were all blondes. Why did I have this abnormality? I knew right then and there, life was going to be a big red challenge.

I have red hair because God knew
I needed a warning label.

My mother was right. I was an anomaly. So far, in my limited six years on earth, I had never seen anyone with hair like mine and I guessed no one else had either. People would stop us in stores while we were shopping or after church and exclaim about the color of my hair, "Is it real?"

Realization Of The Curse

Little ol' ladies would run their arthritic fingers through it and totally creep me out. They would look at my siblings with their blondie locks, then down at me. "Oh, is she adopted?" they would ask. I began to wonder myself.

*Did you know that rubbing a redhead
on the top of the head will bring you good luck?
It might also give you a broken hand, arm, or fingers.*

*They were just jealous that my hair color
could be found in rainbows and theirs
could only be found in dirt!*

My one true friend in those strange early days was my doll, Raggedy Ann. We were inseparable after Santa left her in my care one Christmas morning. I took great care of her, kept her hair tidy and her little dress clean. She even had her own blanket and slept next to

Raggedy Ann

me at night. She listened to my redhead woes and understood because she was also a red head. Although her hair was bright red yarn, she was a true redhead nonetheless.

Never Let A Ginger SNAP

Raggedy didn't freak out when I tied her up in my bike basket and took her for rides down the center line. If she had real fingers, she probably would have given Carl a special salute as we rode swiftly past his name calling.

One day, my sister and I were having a heated discussion about whatever/doesn't matter, and she had had enough. She grabbed Raggedy Ann and called to Dad's springer spaniel hunting dog, Sheba. The dog retrieved ducks and pheasants when hunting with Dad. At home she retrieved sticks and balls. Sheba was all excited, slobbery tongue lolling as she bounded towards us across the front yard.

A Sheba look-alike.

My sister clutched one of Raggedy's legs then waved her around and around over her blondie head. Then she hurled poor Raggedy as far across the yard as she could. I let out a murderously, mournful scream. She issued the command for Sheba to retrieve. The dog shot off, grabbed Raggedy, brought her back to my sister's feet and dropped her in a heap all dog waggily happy waiting for her retrieval treat.

Realization Of The Curse

I was too angry to cry as I grabbed my poor Raggedy. I wanted to swing her at my sister's head, but I couldn't get a good enough grip due to all the dog slobber on Raggedy's beautiful red yarn locks. Sheba's teeth puncture wounds were all across Raggedy's smiling face. I was devastated. My sister was laughing her butt off as I took Raggedy to the house to clean her up and tend to her wounds. Cruelty to us redheads was how I classified this. This was only one of many redhead cruel and traumatic incidents that would follow.

Every Saturday night my mom would wash my sister's golden blondie locks and my red mop. My hair was long and very thick, hard to run a brush through and even more difficult to shampoo. My sister would always go first. Mom saved the battle with me for last. Dad would lift us up, one at a time, onto the kitchen counter and position us on our back so our head was dropped backwards into the sink.

My sister was done in a jiffy without the slightest peep. My turn. I hated it. I screamed bloody murder and kicked my feet. My mother got shampoo in my eyes and ears, water all over herself, the cupboards, and the kitchen window over the sink. I just knew she was trying to drown me. (I believe they now call this form of torture "water boarding" for bad guys and spies.) My father held my legs which made me fight all the more until he hauled off and swatted me. The neighbor lady across the street could hear me screaming for dear life, but never came to my rescue. She would just wave at my mom from her kitchen window then put her hands in the prayer position and look heavenward. Didn't help me a damn bit.

After the hair washing torture. Author on the (L) blondie sister on the (R).

My second hair trauma events occurred at the beauty shop every six weeks. When Mother couldn't get the brush through my hair during my nightly hundred-stroke-brushings, she took me to have my hair "thinned." The poor beautician used every trick in the book to get me to sit still, but I was a brat. She finally resorted to bribery with a sucker. If I would sit still for five minutes, I would get the sucker. She even set a timer! She would be half way through the thinning process and the

Realization Of The Curse

timer would ding. I would happily remain still while I enjoyed the sucker and the job was quickly finished. Seeing my red hair all over the floor was distressing, but those strawberry flavored suckers were really good, even though pieces of my hair might have been stuck to it.

My mother did not believe in kindergarten and there were no preschools in those days. My grandmother taught me how to write my name, my A,B,Cs, and how to count to one hundred; she was a teacher in her younger days. My first day of first grade was terrifying. I still remember the smell of that classroom: a mixture of crisp white paper, mimeograph ink, fresh new books, new sharp crayons, strange carpet, and puke. My stomach was in a clench and wanted to revolt, but I vowed not to puke, no matter what. My legs felt rubbery when I had to stand. My brand new brown saddle shoes pinched my feet and the dress mom made me was too tight around the neck; it felt like I was being strangled at the throat and squeezed to death at the feet. I was a nervous wreck. But I did not puke!

I took a quick look at my classmates as they arrived. Not one kid had red hair or anything close to it. Upon further observations at recess and in the cafeteria for lunch I noted there was not a single redhead in the entire school. After several days/weeks, I also met plenty of Susies, Marys, and Cathys, but not a single Claudia. And to top it all, no one had a weird, hard to pronounce last name like I did. The teacher could never get it right and the kids would giggle when she tried.

The kids stared at me like I was an alien. "What's wrong with your hair?" they would ask. "Do you have the brown measles?" referring to my freckles. "Are you related to Howdy Doody?" "Are you one of those red Commies on the news?" It was a nightmare. I threw a fit every morning, not wanting to return. Finally, Dad said I could ride J.C. to school if I would stop the morning tantrums. He knew my weak spot. He even bought a bigger bike basket for J.C. so my lunch pail and workbooks would fit.

We lived about a mile from the school so this was a huge deal for six year old me. We mapped out my course on streets less travelled with few houses and open pastures between our home and the school. Then we drove the course in the car multiple times. Dad pointed out landmarks, where to make turns, where to stop for traffic, and which houses to stop at if I needed help. Riding rules would be strictly enforced: no more center line riding, both hands on the handlebar grips at all times, and come straight home after school.

Bad weather was no excuse for not riding - my raincoat, rain hat, and boots for rainy days and my snowsuit, itchy wool hat, mittens, and boots for snow. This was a dream come true! Not many kids were allowed to ride their bikes to school, they walked. I then became that girl named Claudia with the strange hair, weird last name, who rode her big green bike to school every day.

There is only one thing redheads cannot do -
be invisible.

Chapter 2

My Redheaded Super Heroes

I have red hair. What's your superpower?

"Say kids, what time is it?" And we all yelled, "It's Howdy Doody Time!" Then we all sang along with the television's Peanut Gallery:

> It's Howdy Doody time,
> It's Howdy Doody time,
> Bob Smith and Howdy, too,
> Say "Howdy do" to you.
> Let's give a rousing cheer
> "Cause Howdy Doody's here.
> It's time to start the show
> So kids, let's go!

Every afternoon at 5:30, our little black and white television was tuned to the local NBC station for *The Howdy Doody Show.* Bob Smith was Buffalo Bob and his little buddy was a marionette named Howdy Doody. Buffalo Bob was like every kid's Grandpa, loved by all. Howdy was a freckle-faced, big eared, wooden boy with red hair. Heidi Doody was his blonde adopted sister,

Buffalo Bob & Howdy Doody.

also a marionette. Clarabell the Clown was a favorite on the show. He was a real human who could not speak so communicated with the characters using mime and honking his horn.

The show was colorized in 1955 and for the first time we kids saw that Howdy had bright red hair! Not only did he have red hair, he also had big brown freckles on his wooden cheeks; one freckle

Howdy Doody checking out his
red hair & brown freckles
on color TV.

for every state in the nation at that time. There were many more characters on the show who collectively taught lessons about human nature and the different kinds of people kids were likely to encounter as they grew older.

Howdy Doody was my hero because he saw the best in everyone despite his hair color, freckles, big ears, wood, and wires. I vowed to be like Howdy in overcoming all future redhead and freckle obstacles. If a wooden dummy could do it, so could I.

(Author's note: On September 24, 1960 Buffalo Bob and Howdy Doody said goodbye to their fans after a historical run of thirteen years and over 2,500 shows on NBC. In a 1975 episode of the popular show, Happy Days, *the original Buffalo Bob and Howdy Doody appeared in a storyline involving Richie Cunningham (Ron Howard). Richie won the Howdy Doody look-alike contest with his (real) red hair and freckles.*

Many present day celebrities began their careers on The Howdy Doody Show. *At one time, Clarabell the Clown was portrayed by Bob Keeshan who later became Captain Kangaroo. A 1954 character on the show, Ranger Bob, later became the Captain of the Star Ship Enterprise, William Shatner.)*

After *The Howdy Doody Show* retired, NBC replaced Saturday morning children's viewing with *The Shari Lewis Show*, in color. Shari was a puppeteer and Lamb Chop seemed to be her favorite puppet character. Shari was a real person

My Redheaded Super Heroes

Shari Lewis & Lamb Chop.

with lovely, real red hair which I greatly admired, but I didn't care much for her show. If she could be a real redhead on television, I would also strive to become a redheaded TV celebrity, too!

Two other television clowns with red hair are worth mentioning. Bozo the clown had ridiculously colored, bright orangish-red hair, weirdly styled. He appeared on a number of children's shows across the United Sates, portrayed by different men in each of the locales. The clown face, costume, and hair were all exactly the same so as not to confuse the young child audiences. In some areas, Bozo hosted his own show, *Bozo's Circus,* with music, dancing, and fun activities for kids. In the Washington, D.C.

television viewing area, Willard Scott played Bozo on WRC-TV for three years (1959-1962) before being replaced by another Bozo. The show's sponsor was McDonald's. I did not like Bozo the clown and still don't. He had creepy red hair and was just plain weird. These days, when we endure someone a little off/weird, we might say, "He is a real Bozo." That is the origination of the phrase.

Bozo the Clown was a real bozo!

In 1963 the former Bozo, Willard Scott, was hired by McDonald's to create and play the role of, "Ronald McDonald, the Hamburger-Happy Clown." Every child in the world now recognizes Ronald McDonald with his poofy red hair, his bright yellow clown suit, striped socks, and giant red shoes. I like Ronald because I like hamburgers, cheese burgers, and big Macs and because Ronald isn't a

Ronald McDonald.

Bozo. Now sing the hamburger song with me: "Two all beef patties, special sauce, lettuce, cheese, pickles, onions on a sesame seed bun!" Then Ronald would say, "It's a good time for the great taste of McDonald's."

(Author's note: Willard Scott performed frequently as Ronald McDonald in the Washington, D.C. area from 1963-1966 with an occasional appearance as late as 1971. He was best known as the weatherman on a local D.C. television station then hired by NBC in 1980 as the weatherman for The Today Show. *Scott announced his retirement on December 11, 2015.* The Today Show *aired a tribute to him on his final day, December 15, which featured multiple clips of his antics with them over the past many years. The plaza outside of Rockefeller Center was renamed Willard Scott Way in his honor.)*

Watch Mr. Wizard was another inspirational show, not because he was redheaded, but because he was a scientist and encouraged girls to have an interest in science. Every Saturday morning I tuned in to watch a boy or girl visit Mr. Wizard (Don Herbert). One of the young girls that visited Mr. Wizard on a regular basis was Rita McLaughlin, a

Mr. Wizard with two of his assistants.

redhead! She always asked intelligent questions and took an active part in the experiments. The young visitors would learn some amazing scientific fact on each show by working an experiment with Mr. Wizard in his laboratory. The experiments were very simple and could be recreated by viewers at home, especially with the "Fun With the Mr. Wizard Science Set." I begged for the set after joining the "Mr. Wizard Science Club" and set up my

Fun with Mr. Wizard Science Set.

own "lab" in our basement. The Set had a microscope, which was pretty cheesy in what it could accomplish, but I was happily looking at bugs, flowers, leaves, hair strands, and spit under magnification. Science was an eye opener for me and I wanted to pursue it.

(Author's note: Watch Mr. Wizard *received high ratings and awards with millions of viewers each week, young and old alike. There were 5,000 Mr. Wizard Science Clubs by 1955 and 50,000 by 1965. The television show itself was cited by the National Science foundation and American Chemical Society for increasing interest in science. The show also won the Peabody Award in 1953. The last telecast was June 27, 1965. The young redhead, Rita McLaughlin, went on to become a successful actress. She was actress Patty Duke's double on* The Patty Duke Show, *then later starred on the television soap opera,* As The World Turns *for many years.)*

My dad loved aviation. We went to all the nearby airshows and marveled at the military displays and jet teams, aerobatic performances, low level fast passes, formation flying, and the parachute teams. On television, he liked to watch

Sky King with us kids. The show was a western-themed adventure featuring an airplane pilot-cowboy type who helped local law enforcement catch bad guys, solve mysteries, and find lost people. Sky King did these things every week in just 30 minutes on black-and-white television. I just liked to watch Sky fly the airplane, a twin engine Cessna he called Songbird.

Sky King and Penny aboard the Songbird.

Sky had a niece (Penny) and nephew (Clipper) living with him on the Flying Crown Ranch. Penny was my idol. Since the show was not in color, it was difficult to see if she was a redhead (she was a blonde). Whether she was or not, she was young, very polite, well mannered, but bold and daring; just like a redhead would be. She was an accomplished pilot who participated in air races and was licensed to fly multiengine aircraft like the Songbird. Penny and Sky were a great influence on girls and boys at that time. Many went on to become pilots and a few became astronauts as a result of watching the show. Not only could men fly aircraft, women were perfectly capable of doing the same.

(Author's note: The Sky King *show lasted until 1959, all episodes filmed in black-and-white. Although the series was set in Arizona it was actually filmed in the high desert of California, specifically the areas in and around Apple Valley, China Lake (the Naval Air Weapons Station), and the San Bernardino Mountains. Interior settings were filmed in Hollywood studios. Because of the aircraft, vehicles, fuel, and multiple film sets, the budget, at that time, was fairly expensive for what was deemed a children's show - nearly $9,000 per episode. When not filming, Penny (Gloria Winters) and Sky (Kirby Grant) performed as a song-and-dance team at State fairs and signed autographs after their routines. At a fair in Dallas, Texas, four fans of the show waited patiently in line with their children for autographs. Those fans were future astronauts Gus Grissom, Pete Conrad, Alan Shepard, and Wally Schirra.)*

When I saw the *Wizard of Oz* movie for the first time, I was enchanted by Glinda the good witch. She was dazzling in her magnificent gown and jeweled crown. She was kind to everyone and

Glinda the good witch
in the Wizard of Oz.

had the sweetest voice. Her magic wand saved the ruby slippers from the wicked witch who had been squished under the fallen house. The slippers were somehow magically placed on Dorothy's feet. Toward the end of the movie, Glinda appears for the last time to save the day for Dorothy. She helped with more magic wand waving as she chanted: "There's no place like home, there's no place like home…"

Glinda, played by actress Billie Burke, was one of my heroines because, not only was she kind,

My Redheaded Super Heroes

helpful, beautiful, and magical, she had gorgeous red hair.

One of my favorite heroines from childhood to present day was Amelia Earhart. Just like me, she had freckles, red hair, a split between her two front teeth, and she loved to fly. She set multiple flying records in a variety of aircraft, didn't seem to put up with negativity from anyone, made her own decisions... She helped all young and older redheaded girls dare to be brave and follow their dreams despite the bullies in the world. I wanted to be like Amelia, a daring and brave pilot.

Amelia Earhart.

I knew from an early age that I would become a nurse. My Aunt Betty, whom I admired greatly, was a nurse and worked her way up the ladder to become a hospital administrator. My Great-aunt Mary was also a nurse. In the early 1900s, she was instrumental in establishing a nursing school at one of the first large hospitals in Spokane, Washington. My nursing destiny was set in my DNA. When I wasn't watching redheads on television I was reading about nurses. The "Cherry Ames" series of fiction books were my favorites even though the cover pictures always showed Cherry with black hair. I was sure that with a name like "Cherry" and all of her adventures, she should have had red hair. Nonetheless, the stories were very influential toward my future nursing career.

Cherry Ames Student Nurse book.

When I read about Florence Nightingale and Clara Barton, I was thrilled to see that Florence was a redhead (Clara was a brunette). Florence was very stubborn and opinionated; a typical redhead. Both women were trailblazers and I was destined to become a nurse trailblazer, too.

At my nursing school graduation ceremony, the entire class held little lamps with a candle symbolizing Florence, the Lady with the Lamp, as we all recited the Nightingale Pledge.

Some people outgrow childish shenanigans…
redheads master them.

Chapter 3

I Am A Mutant Anomaly - Really

*Real red hair doesn't come in a bottle,
it's in your genes!*

When people would exclaim over the color of my hair and impolitely ask, "Where did she get that hair?" my mother would smile, pat me on the head and reply, "She was my first. I had rusty pipes." We would then briskly walk away while the inquisitor tried to think of a response. Not until I took high school biology did I understand completely how that could not have been true!

On the other hand, my father would begin by saying I was conceived from an alien being and go into great detail about UFOs, flying saucers, and the "grays" in the Pacific Northwest. To this day, there is a teeny tiny bit of (foolish) anxious wonder on my part about this, and here's why:

During WWII, pilots in all theaters of combat, frequently reported sightings of unidentified flying objects (UFOs). The strange objects flew at tremendous speeds, followed aircraft, were seen night and day, but rarely displayed hostile behavior. Pilots and their crews called them, <u>foo-fighters</u>.

Never Let A Ginger SNAP

On June 24, 1947 near Mt. Rainier in Washington State, Kenneth Arnold, a well-respected pilot and local Boise, Idaho businessman, was flying his single engine aircraft to Yakima on a business trip. A bright flash of light caught his eye, followed by a second flash. He turned to observe a string of nine shiny round objects flying an echelon formation in a southeasterly direction.

Kenneth Arnold.

They seemed to follow alongside him for a few seconds then darted down and through the valleys near the base of Mt.Rainier, finally disappearing altogether behind the mountain. He calculated their speed at just under 1,700 miles per hour which was three times faster than any manned aircraft in 1947 and way beyond supersonic speed, at that. He thought maybe they were secret experimental aircraft from the nearby Boeing plant near Seattle.

(Author's note: Normal speed of sound is 768+ mph. The sound barrier was broken by Chuck Yeager on October 14, 1947 in an X-1 rocket. At

an altitude of 40,000 feet, the speed of sound is 662 mph, which he successfully reached.)

News of Arnold's observation quickly spread to the news media. This was the first non-military reported post-war sighting in the United States of unidentified flying objects. Arnold described the unknowns as saucer or disc shaped. At that time, the term "flying saucers" was credited to him by the news media.

Kenneth Arnold with an artist rendering of the UFOs he saw.

A few weeks later, July 8, 1947, news media reported multiple UFOs had crashed outside of Roswell, New Mexico. The military quickly covered the story by issuing press statements and pictures of a crashed weather balloon to avoid mass panic.

Press photo of Jesse Marcel with pieces of a "weather balloon."

There were multiple top secret government projects for the war effort taking place in the mid-1940s. One of the most top secret of all was the Manhattan Project with multiple operational sites across the United States. At the Hanford, Washington site, plutonium was produced for the atomic bombs that would later be dropped on Japan. The finished plutonium was then sent to Los Alamos, New Mexico for weapons testing. Both of these sites secretly documented frequent sightings of UFOs passing over or hovering above the sites.

In July 1945, six F6F Hellcat fighter planes were alerted to intercept a large UFO hovering over one of the reactors at Hanford. The day was bright and clear, blue sky, no clouds. All six of the Hellcat pilots reported visual contact with the unknown flying object. They described it as the size of three aircraft carriers side-by-side, oval shaped, and emitting a cloud like vapor from around its outer edges. The craft hovered over the reactor for nearly twenty minutes before it shot straight up to an altitude of 65,000 feet and disappeared from sight.

There have been thousands more sightings around the world which continue to present day, but let us return to my father and his story of my creation. First, recall the dates of nearby documented sightings in Washington State: June,

July 1947. I was likely conceived in August 1947, born in April 1948.

The Hanford nuclear site is about two hundred miles southwest of Fairfield, Washington where my family farmed. Eastern Washington is farming country with thousands and thousands of acres growing wheat, lentils, peas, and barley during that time. Farmers out in their fields from sunup to sundown frequently spotted UFOs zooming overhead. My father was one of those farmers. Most kept their sightings to themselves for fear of ridicule by the non-believers, but not my dad. He called them The Visitors. He said that when they were zipping around the buttes and flying low to the ground they were likely challenging each other or goofing off like teenagers would do in their cars. If the larger crafts were moving slowly at a higher altitude, they were likely observing. I always wondered how he knew that or was he just making it up? When questioned, he would just smile and shrug his shoulders.

One night while spending the weekend at my grandparent's Fairfield farmhouse, I was awakened by the farm dogs barking viciously, as if an intruder was approaching. The house was in the middle of nowhere surrounded by acres and acres of wheat. Any car or person, night or day, could be spotted coming up the road from quite a distance out. It was pitch black outside, likely way past midnight. I went to the window, pushed it up and listened for a car crunching on the gravel driveway. Nothing, just the dogs going crazy, worse than usual for an intruder. Something was...

Suddenly, the dogs stopped mid-bark with a little yip. There was dead silence. Not even a cricket cricking. The hair was suddenly standing up on the back of my neck. My stomach was a bit queasy for no apparent reason. As I recall, I believe I was about eight years old at that time.

BOOM! The most brilliant white light you could ever imagine instantly blinded me. I stepped back from the window to cover my eyes. The entire two-story house was completely enveloped in this powerful light. There was no sound whatsoever, until... a soft purring sound came from above. I was holding my breath, not moving a single muscle, heart crashing in my chest, stomach trying not to puke. As soon as I heard that soft, reassuring sound, I relaxed and let out my breath. It was just The Visitors, again. The light suddenly snapped off and I was once again blinded, this time by darkness.

The next morning I told dad, "The Visitors were here again last night with their light. Got the dogs all upset." He put his fingers to his lips and made the shhh sign, "Don't say anything to Grandma, she gets all upset. I saw it too. They were just checking on you." Then he would chuckle. Really, Dad?

In 1982 when *E.T. the Extra-Terrestrial* movie debuted, I wondered if E.T. was my cousin. He didn't have red hair or freckles though and the poor little thing was really ugly, in a cute sort of way.

E. T.

Do you understand why I remain a bit skeptical about my origin, based on my father's birds-n-bees discussions?! Of course, my mother always denied this wild tale. She would just shake her head and say dad drank too many martinis. High school biology was also helpful in dispelling this myth... kinda.

Let's take a look at the real history of where we redheads came from.

You can't buy the fire, you are born with it.

For an interesting look at the real origin of redheads, read *Red - A History Of The Redhead* by Jacky Colliss Harvey. She explores the history as far back as Adam and Eve. I do not intend to go that far back in our history, instead I'll just touch on the high points for you.

Contrary to common belief, redheads did not originate in Scotland nor in Ireland. We are descendants from Africa and the Central Asian grasslands 35,000 to 40,000 years ago. Some of our more adventurous ancestors set out to explore beyond their homelands ending up in what is now Europe and Russia. Those long ago ancestors had dark skin, dark hair, and eyes. They had the ability to tolerate strong sunlight without horrific sunburn damage.

The further north those ancestors moved, the more their bodies had to adapt to environmental changes. Northern regions do not have the harsh sunlight and desert-like conditions their ancestors experienced. Skin and hair evolved becoming lighter and lighter. Eyes became lighter in color in order to see better in less sunlight. Evolution and mutations in their genes over thousands and thousands of years caused these changes to protect them and assist in living longer in their strange new environments.

As the skin became lighter, it began to synthesize its own Vitamin D. Vitamin D is naturally synthesized when our skin is exposed to sunlight. Since there is less exposure to sunlight in the Northern regions, their bodies adapted by becoming able to synthesize Vitamin D faster with shorter sunlight exposure. Those with darker skin needed longer exposure to make the same amount of Vitamin D. Without adequate Vitamin D, bones would become soft and more susceptible to injuries, rickets, arthritis, and other maladies. Our ancestors would not have been able to survive and evolve without the capability of maintaining strong bones.

The genetic mutations that took place over those thousands of years ago while our ancestors migrated to the Northern regions is known as genetic drift. This explains how folks in Scotland and Ireland have the lighter hair, skin, and eyes we see now. Genetic drift caused the evolution of genetic mutations which helped them adapt and survive the Northern environments.

Was there one specific gene that miraculously had a mind of its own and mutated in so many ways over so many generations that it gave us redheads all of our quirks? YES!

I am an MC1R mutant.

Chromosomes are microscopic structures within our cells that contain our genes. They have long strands of DNA and contain hundreds, sometimes thousands, of genes.

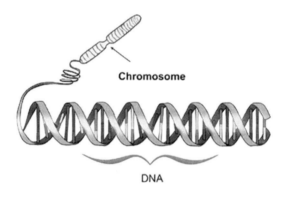

Everyone has a chromosome #16 which contains 800-900 genes each providing the instructions for making proteins. Different proteins perform a variety of roles in the body, for example: hair and eye color, skin tones, height, and hundreds more.

Redheads have a mutated gene on their chromosome #16. This mutation was identified in 1995 by Professor Jonathan Rees of the

I Am A Mutant Anomaly - Really

Department of Dermatology at the University of Edinburgh. He was undertaking a study of the DNA from people with and without red hair to determine whether there was any type of genetic difference. Rees and his team of researchers were inspired by an earlier 1993 genetic study of yellow characteristics in mice undertaken by scientist Roger Cone. The yellow mice had the same imbalance of two chromosomes also commonly found in humans with red hair. When the advanced studies began, Rees' team expected to find only one or two variants in the gene. They initially found over twenty! The team was so surprised they actually thought their machines had malfunctioned. Further studies began to determine what each variant of the mutated gene was responsible for.

Prof. Jonathan Rees.

One of those mutated genes on #16 is the Melanocortin 1 Receptor or MC1R for short. Scientifically and microscopically speaking, MC1R is a seven-pass G-coupled receptor at chromosome 16q24.3, or in layman's terms, our red hair's postal address along with zip code.

How does this MC1R gene make us redheads "mutants"? The MC1R gene itself is a mutant that can be broken down into over 400 possible variants. One of those variants blocks the production of <u>eumelanin</u> (the pigment for dark brown and black hair with brown eyes) which causes a buildup of <u>phaeomelanin</u> (the pigment for blond and red hair with lighter colored eyes).

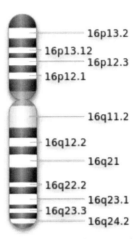

The #16 Melanocortin 1 Receptor gene. Note the bottom location of 16q24.2

The degree of the phaeomelanin buildup determines the variety of shades we see in redheads, from strawberry blonde to copper tones to deep rusty auburn. The more phaeomelanin you have built up, the more vibrant your red shade will be. The balance between the eumelanin and phaeomelanin also determines the body's ability to tan versus freckle. Still being investigated are the effects of the highest levels of phaeomelanin which may produce other dangerous mutations when exposed to UV radiation. Stay tuned and watch for those study results.

Another variant of the MC1R gene also appears in endothelial cells, in the lining of the blood vessels, and in immune cells involved in the blood clotting process; a likely explanation why redheads seem to bleed and bruise more than others. More on this topic later.

These are just a couple of the variants attributed to the MC1R gene from the 400 identified. It will take years to figure out every single one and what actions they have on us. Ongoing discussion of mutations for this one particular chromosome could fill an entire book and make any reader (and the author) a bit batty. Clearly, we redheads are mutants for sure! Let's move forward and learn about heredity.

Keep calm and rock it like a redhead.

Chapter 4

The Red Inheritance

Red Hair - the crown you never take off.

My paternal grandma was fair skinned, had a hint of rusty colored hair, and blue eyes. She loved my hair. I would sit on the floor in front of her chair while she brushed my hair and listened to her tell me Bible stories. (She taught Sunday School and practiced the lessons on me she was to give.) On occasion, while she brushed away, I would tell her about the teasing and taunts I endured from the school kids and that stupid neighbor kid, Carl. She would smile and tell me those kids were just jealous. "They didn't know how to express how much they admired how pretty your hair is." Hmmm, well that was certainly a different perspective. She also told me that Carl likely had a crush on me. EEEWWW, yuck. He was a creepy little jerk! "Tsk, tsk," she would say and match my concern with the appropriate Bible story.

One day she told me Carl only came out on his porch because he had to wear leg braces as a result of having polio (remember, this was the late 1950s). I felt bad hearing that. I knew several kids my age who had survived the terrible disease but

The Red Inheritance

became crippled as a result and had to wear leg braces to help them walk.

(Author's note: The most serious polio epidemics occurred in the summers during the 1940s and 1950s. Polio vaccines became available in 1955 (injections) and 1961 (oral). Due to the success of the vaccines, polio has been eradicated in the United States since 1979.)

No wonder we never saw Carl outside playing or riding a bike. Grandma gave me a big bag full of her delicious cookies and told me to go knock on Carl's front door and offer to share. "Be nice. Get to know him. See what happens," she said.

Everyone needs a smart-ass sarcastic redhead
in their life.

Turns out, Carl was really a nice kid, a musical prodigy, and yes, he was fascinated with my hair. He was very lonely, an only child, and other kids were afraid of his braces and walking difficulties so they made fun of him. We were both oddities to others. He stopped calling me carrot top and switched to rusty. I called him clink because his braces made clinky sounds when he walked. He became one of my best kid friends for several years until we had to move away.

Grandma was right. She always told me my hair was my crowning glory, a blessing from God, and to never doubt what He had intended for me. "Red hair is your built-in strength and courage," she exclaimed, time and again. I rather liked this theory. It wasn't rusty pipes or out-of-this-world.

It's not just a hair color,
it's a state of mind.

So how does that MC1R gene give me this hair or, as grandma believes, how and why did God do this to me?

Ninety percent of the world's population has brown, black, or blonde hair, in that dominant order. Less than 1-2% of people worldwide have red hair. That percentage rises by 2-6% of the population north of the equator. Scotland has the highest proportion of redheads at 13%, followed by Ireland at 10%. The United States has only a 2-6% proportion of redheads; however, by population concentration worldwide, the U.S. has the largest at 6-18 million redheads. There are more redheaded women in the world than redheaded men.

The Red Inheritance

Those with present day Norseman or Viking heritage are blue-eyed redheads. Genetic analysis suggests red hair in Norway, Denmark, and Sweden was brought back from Ireland and Scotland by 9th century Viking raiders. The gene was then passed through centuries of generations. Consequently, most redheaded men have blue eyes. Those raiding Viking rascals!

Blood types are also significant when discussing genetic heritage. The majority (51%) of Scots have the O+ blood type; 34% have A+; 12% B+; 3% have AB+ which is fairly rare.

Irish blood types are most commonly O+ (47%) followed by A+ (26%). AB- is the least common.

The United States melting pot records O+ (37%) and A+ (35%).

Several researched articles note redheads have a higher likelihood of Rh- blood type due to the MC1R gene (both are recessive traits). In a very unscientific poll undertaken by this author of over 400 true redheads from a variety of countries, the results were as follows: 194 were A+; 44 were A-; 42 were B+; 19 were B-; 40 were AB+; 14 were AB-; 121 were O+; and 123 were O-. Types A+, O+, and O- were the most common, as expected. Two hundred redheads were, in fact, Rh-; 50% of the group. This <u>un</u>scientific research may or may not prove anything, but was interesting to the author and fun for the participants nonetheless!

(This redheaded author with Scot/Irish/English heritage has A+ blood type. Do you know your blood type? You should!)

Forty percent of people (or 4 in 10) carry the MC1R gene, but only 1-2% of carriers produce a redhead. A British genetic testing company found that in the UK alone there were 20 million MC1R gene carriers even though only 4% of the population actually has red hair. Those who carry the gene but never produce a redhead may be termed by the scientists as <u>secret</u> <u>gingers</u>. The gene will continue to be passed from generation to generation, but not all generations will produce a redhead. The folk belief that redheads "skip" a generation is untrue. It's all in the genes and how they match. Check this out:

* If **both** parents carry the MC1R gene they have a **100%** chance of producing a redhead.
* If one parent is a **redhead** and the other parent is a **carrier**, but not a redhead, they have a **50%** chance of producing a redhead.
* If **both** parents are **carriers** but not redheads,

The Red Inheritance

they have a **25%** chance of producing a red-head.

* If one parent is a **carrier** and the other parent is a **non carrier** they have a **0%** chance of having a redhead.

AWWHAA! That explains it! Both my parents carried the MC1R gene. My mother was a redhead, my dad was not, but he was fair skinned with light brown hair, so I am a 50% chancer! But wait, how come my siblings don't have red hair? Are we back to the alien theory?

Recall the MC1R gene can have over 400 variants. Those variants determine not only hair color, but also eye color, hand dominance, skin tones, and more. Genes are either recessive or dominant. MC1R is a recessive gene. Recessive traits come in pairs. Recessive traits are blue eyes (only 17% of people worldwide have blue eyes), fair skin, freckles, and left handedness.

Okay now, stay with me here. The majority of redheads worldwide have brown, hazel, or green eyes in that order of dominance. Those dominant eye color traits apparently did not hook up with the recessive MC1R as its pair. Likewise, if you are a redhead without fair skin or freckles you missed out in the recessive vs dominant traits hook up on the MC1R. Your darker skin trait is dominant over the recessive fair skin trait - lucky you! You might be able to tan in the sun instead of burn and peel.

On the other hand, or the recessive trait pairing, if you are a redhead (MC1R) with blue eyes (recessive) you have the rarest combination of recessive pairs in the world. The odds of having red hair **and** blue eyes is around 0.17%. WOW!

A blue eyed redhead.
The perfect blend of fire & ice.

Another recessive trait is left handedness. Only 10-25% of people worldwide are lefties. Right-hander genes are dominant. So, if you are a redhead (MC1R) that hooked up with the leftie recessive you are rare! What if you are a blue-eyed leftie with red hair? WOW, you are weirdly rare! Actually, your MC1R recessive hooked up with either the blue eyed recessive for the pair or your fair skin recessive may have hooked up with your leftie recessive for the pair or the fair skin and blue eyes hooked up or… it's complicated with those 400 possibilities. Just deal with it! You are definitely a rare mutant! We are all mutants!

With all this genetic knowledge (or confusion) I think I have figured out why my sister has blonde hair, blue eyes, and tans in the sun. My one brother has brownish/blonde, blue eyes, fair skin, burns in the sun. My other brother was a towhead (nearly white hair), blue eyes, and tans in the sun. None of us are lefties. It was all determined individually in the MC1R gene with the recessives hooking up with the recessives and the amounts of eumelanin and phaeomelanin challenging each other, I guess. Did I get that right? Google it!

When life gives you red hair -
rock it, own it, embrace it.

Chapter 5

Hairy History Horrors

The maiden with the flaming red hair
is as fierce as she is fair.

It was in high school American History class where I was devastated to learn about the Salem Witch Trials. Our football coach/history teacher briefly touched on the subject as there were only one or two paragraphs mentioned in our history textbook reading assignment. I was onto his tricks of throwing test questions at us about subjects mentioned in short paragraphs or page highlights, so I paid close attention to the information about the Salem witches.

During football season, he gave essay assignments on Wednesdays, due the following Monday. We could work on our essays in class Thursday and Friday while he worked at his desk drawing circles, making notes, and shuffling papers. Football games were on Thursday and Friday nights. Do you see any correlation there? We were to write at least three pages on any subject he had discussed that week. I decided to learn more about the Salem Witch Trials for my essay assignment so a trip to the library was necessary. (There were no computers in those days for Google searches, just the card catalog and plowing through a stack of history books.)

Beginning in January 1692 in the Puritan settlement of Salem, Massachusetts, a group of young girls ages four to seventeen began having "fits" of violent contortions and actions, strange foaming at the mouth, hallucinations, strange language, and blood curdling screams. This behavior had never been witnessed before by the Puritan people. The village doctor had no diagnostic clue as to the cause of all this, other than to declare the young girls must be victims of black magic or possessed by the devil. Fear and hysteria ensued.

Several local women, labeled as "different," were immediately accused of casting black magic spells on the girls using witchcraft. Some of those women where social outcasts to the Puritan community only because they did not follow the Puritan beliefs or rules. Others were quiet, somewhat withdrawn from the community, grew beautiful, bountiful gardens, used herbs and roots to heal the sick, rarely complied with the dress or hair length codes, and had slightly different physical appearances from the other Puritan women. Because they were different from the others, they were deemed witches. Guess what hair color some of those women had? RED! A cold chill ran down my spine when I discovered this fact. I was different too. I had red hair. Was I a witch? I always did like Halloween. Gulp.

The Salem Witch Trials.

Trials began in February. From then through May of 1693, over two hundred women and children, along with six men, and two dogs were accused of witchcraft in and around Salem. Nineteen women and five men were found guilty and hung on Gallows Hill. Thirty were found not guilty and released, but shunned by the community from then on. When a verdict could not be reached, the accused were chained in squalid dungeon-like cellars for several months to years. Five died in the dungeon. Among those chained in the dungeon was a two year old girl who was finally released to her parents after several months. All those held in the dungeon proclaimed their innocence to no avail.

On September 19, 1692 Giles Corey, an 81 year old accused farmer, refused to enter a plea of guilt or innocence at his trial. His punishment was *pein forte et dure*; the French legal term for

Giles Corey's punishment was
pein forte et dure.

hard and forceful punishment. That punishment was torture - he was basically squished to death.

Within public view he was restrained on a platform. Large heavy stones were then placed on his chest in order to elicit a plea. He adamantly refused. This torture continued for two days by adding more and more stones until he finally died from suffocation and fractured ribs which likely punctured his lungs. Squished.

The two dogs were also accused of being possessed by the devil via an act of witchcraft and were put to death.

Present day medical and psychological explanations of what caused the "bewitchment" of the Salem children range from epilepsy, psychological hysteria, mental illness, or encephalitis. The explanation that makes the most sense is convulsive ergotism caused by eating rye bread. The rye grain may have been infected by a fungus. That fungus is a natural substance from which the hallucinogenic drug LSD is derived. They were tripping on LSD? Wow man! Far out! But very sad for all those innocents put to death.

Those punishments were all pretty gruesome and made me ill to think that people would do this to their fellow human beings and animals. As I continued to study, I was even more horrified to find what history had recorded about "different" women throughout Europe into the 1700s.

Medieval laws during those times stipulated that malevolent witchcraft was to be punished by fire to cleanse society of all witches. Germany, Italy, Scotland, France, and Scandinavia experienced witch-hunt hysteria which peaked between the 15th and 18th centuries. Witch hunters preyed upon redheads due to their rarity and easy to find targets. The red hair was thought to indicate an affiliation with the devil, satanic practices, and supernatural powers. Over 50,000 people had been hunted, accused, and executed - more women than men.

Once accused, the victims may have undergone tests to determine if they were in fact witches or to prove their innocence. One such ordeal was the "swimming test." The accused was dragged to a nearby lake or river, stripped to their underwear, hands and feet bound, a rope tied securely around the waist then bodily thrown into the water. The thought process was that an innocent would sink like a rock while a guilty would float (shouldn't that be the other way around?). When it occurred to the "testers" that the innocent had been underwater for awhile and didn't float back to the surface, they yanked her back up and dragged her drowned body back to shore. Oops, I guess she was innocent after all.

Another test, of sorts, was to search the accused for a "witch mark." Besides having red

Examination of a suspected witch.

hair, there was an even more definitive sign. Supposedly, when the witch made her pact with the devil he left a mark somewhere on her body. Freckles, moles, birthmarks, and scars were all considered as proof of the witch mark(s). The accused was stripped naked publicly and thoroughly examined. Besides the freckles as proof, the true redhead would have red pubic hair

Hairy History Horrors

which was an obvious sign she had been "touched down there" by the devil. GUILTY.

Others believed those with red hair had stolen fires from hell and must surely be witches. Therefore, the accused should be returned to the fires; they would be burned to death. Once found guilty, the accused witch was first hanged or beheaded then burned to ashes to protect the innocent from post mortem sorcery. Some cultures tied the live accused to a stake in the center of a huge pile of wood, garbage, or other combustible items, and set ablaze. This was done in the center of the village for all to witness the horrific and agonizing death.

The ancient Greeks believed those with red hair would turn into vampires upon their death. Whether they were witches or not, the Greeks would not chance vampires when any redhead died. Her body was immediately burned to ashes.

My essay for the high school history class, as well as my abbreviated history here, was an eye opener. It also assured me that I was not imagining things when people stopped and stared or made derogatory comments about my hair. It also made me wonder if I had any witchcraft genes attached to that MC1R critter. I knew I had superpowers, just didn't broadcast them. But I knew of others with superpowers who did.

P.S. I received an A+ on that history essay!

If you see a redhead - approach gingerly.

Chapter 6

Paranormal Superpowers

*Redheads are born with superpowers,
they just don't realize they possess them.*

My maternal grandmother always had a pink cloud around her. My paternal grandmother always had a brilliant green cloud around her. Dad was sometimes surrounded by pale green or a bluish color. Mother was greenish-brownish depending on her mood. My grammar school friends rarely had bright colored clouds except for Clink, aka Carl. When he was playing the piano he was in his element, full of joy. He had a bright, almost blindingly gold cloud that seemed to pulsate around him. I was always amazed to see that.

One day I was helping my maternal grandmother work in her rose garden. We were talking about how she propagated roses to create her own varieties. As she talked, her cloud became brighter and brighter. I told her, "You sure are pink today!" She stopped what she was doing, looked at me and said, "You can see my aura?" That was another moment when I learned I was not like others.

Grandma told me everyone has an aura, but only special people can see them. An aura is an individual's energy field. It looks like a misty cloud or halo. It colorizes the energy being given off by that individual. A person's aura color can tell a lot about that individual - their personality, vitality, emotions, spiritual awareness, and more.

I was intrigued by what she told me. I thought everyone saw the colors. She started asking me all kinds of questions about things that I experienced everyday. Did I dream I was flying; where did I go? Could I hear people's thoughts or know what would happen before it happened? Could I sense when someone or an animal was distressed or sick? I answered her questions with my own, "Doesn't everyone do that or see that, or experience that?" "No," was her reply, "you are special, just like your hair. You must learn what these gifts are and how to use them as you get older."

Many years later, as a teen, my mother and I attended a housewarming party for one of her work friends. I had never met any of those people, I was just along for the ride and the likelihood of some good potluck food. As we entered the living room, I was immediately drawn to the most beautiful woman I had ever seen sitting in a large overstuffed chair. She had long, silky, jet black hair, porcelain white skin, and the most brilliant, vibrating, purple aura. I had never seen anyone with a purple aura; it drew me to her like a magnet. She held her arms out to me as I approached and said, "I've been waiting for you." I'm sure that would have creeped anyone else out, but I felt as if I had known her forever as my best friend. She told me her name was Sylvi. When I was in middle school I had named my diary, Sylvi. Prophetic? Creepy? Just plain weird? All of those?

We sat and talked until the party had way past ended and clean up had begun. She told me I had "untapped powers" and would teach me how to use them. I told her that my grandmother had said the same thing when I was younger and I would learn more as I grew older. Sylvi was my teacher.

Sylvi explained that it was very common for redheads to be psychic in a number of ways. We should only fear those gifts if used in hurtful or harmful ways. Since I was to become a nurse (how did she know that?) I would use those gifts everyday to help and heal. And I certainly did.

One day, in my college psychology class, our teacher introduced us to a student who was studying metaphysics at the nearby university. The student wanted to try a couple of experiments on us for a paper he was writing. Our class of nearly thirty agreed to participate.

He wanted to test us on our ESP (Extra Sensory Perception) abilities. He had a deck of Zener cards for testing ESP which he quickly shuffled in front of us. Each Zener card has a single figure on it of either a square, a circle, a star, a plus sign, or wavy lines. He would look at the

card, close his eyes, and picture it in his mind. We were to write down what we thought he was seeing. After he finished the deck, he polled the class on how many each of us had correctly identified. A few missed all of them; a few got a couple of them; one or two got more than five correct. When he asked if anyone got more than ten correct, one boy raised his hand and so did I. The boy had eleven correct. I had twenty-five correct - all of them. I thought our tester's eyeballs would roll out of his head. "REALLY? You got all of them?" he was stunned. We repeated the experiment with nearly the same results for everyone, including mine. Class was dismissed. He asked if I would stay a moment and talk to him. He was so excited that I had scored perfectly both times, he wasn't quite sure how to proceed. Whatever his theory was, I guess I blew it all to hell. I became a volunteer guinea pig for further testing at the university. He wrote his paper and earned a high mark while I earned a headache after all that mind reading.

Years later while working in the emergency room as an RN, one of my abilities was to see a bright red spot on a patient's body indicating a problem. I called them hot spots. I could only see these when I was fully rested and energized. I never told anyone (fellow nurses or physicians) why I suspected something specific when I saw them, only suggested we should take a closer look. This proved a curse at times, trying to convince the physician(s) that I suspected something not clearly visible upon examination

Claudia Hagen, RN.

nor confirmed by lab work. I'm sure they thought I was nuts, but I was nearly always correct.

After multiple times of positive results when my suspicions/suggestions proved correct, one of the physicians pulled me aside and asked, point blank, "How do you always seem to know?" My dilemma was how to explain without making him think I was some sort of witch-nurse-doctor. The entire crew already knew my trick of predicting when the phone would ring or a specific emergency would come through the door. I always brushed it off by saying, "Anyone can do that. It just takes practice." Which is true; we all possess the capability, redheads even more so.

I decided to tell that particular physician how I frequently saw hot spots which nearly always indicated a problem; the intensity of the red color correlated with the severity of the problem. He didn't laugh at me nor question the ability. He just thanked me for telling him. That wasn't the end of it.

One evening, a woman law enforcement officer in her mid-thirties came in complaining of extreme fatigue to the point of feeling she would pass out. She did not feel safe going on duty and needed a note from a doctor in order to call in sick.

She was very pale, blood pressure was low, no fever, no complaint of any specific pain. She had the brightest red pulsating spot over her left lower abdomen I had ever seen. Everything about this woman set off my alarm bells. I pulled that particular physician aside who knew my talent(?) and told him what I saw. It was not appendicitis - wrong side, no pain. Lab reports came back normal. She was a bit dehydrated. It was a puzzle. I insisted he order an abdominal x-ray. He retaliated with the concern there was no solid evidence for the insurance to see the validity in paying for it. I insisted there was something terribly wrong with this young woman and it needed immediate attention. I finally told him the hot spot was the brightest I'd ever seen and begged, "Please, please, order an abdominal x-ray." He finally relented.

The x-ray showed a huge left ovarian mass. After more specific tests, the mass proved to be stage four ovarian cancer.

Never underestimate the superpowers of a redhead.

Redheads have been known to possess a heightened intuition and awareness of their surroundings. We operate differently from non-redheads. In multiple studies of psychic ability, redheads consistently proved to have 14% more intuitiveness than a base measurement of non-redheads. Redheads are naturally gifted with ESP due to their sensitivity to the environment, particularly nature. Psychic skills are heightened by the ability to process either physical or emotional sensory data. These abilities are present in early childhood. As the child ages the influence of peers and adults to become less sensitive, less emotional, less dependent on spirituality, deters their further development of psychic skills. Without practice, the skills are most often lost.

Because redheads have a heightened awareness of their physical and emotional surroundings, they are often termed, empaths. Not all empaths are redheads, but chances are highly likely redheads possess the abilities to become more skilled than non-reds, if they would simply pursue and practice their gift(s).

Is there a difference between an empath and an intuitive or psychic? They are similar, yet differ.

Empaths are born and may or may not work hard to improve their skills. They are highly sensitive to those around them often able to sense what others are thinking or feeling, including pain. They find comfort in nature, music, and art. An empath uses her gift to always help others; nurses are empaths whether they realize it or not. Most empaths are women. If you were a *Star Trek: The Next Generation* fan, recall the character, Officer Deanna Troi. She portrayed an empath and in some scenes she was shown with long curly red hair.

Officer Deanna Troi, the ship's empath.

The term psychic often conjures a vision of a gypsy with her crystal ball, the old time snake oil salesman, or the television entertainers who talk to the deceased. Some are real, some actually possess the skills, while some are total money seeking quacks. Those with the true gifts are highly intuitive due to their ability to process sensory data on an emotional, physical or spiritual level. They have developed their skills to help others in a variety of ways. Everyone is born with intuition - that "gut feeling," that little voice of consciousness - but few choose to develop and utilize it.

Are you a redheaded empath or an intuitive? Figure it out for yourself. Which list do you identify with (maybe both?):

Empath

1. Feels others emotions as if their own.
2. Often overwhelmed in public or crowded areas.
3. Knowing when someone is lying or being dishonest. Strives for truth in all things.
4. Has a history of digestive disorders and lower back problems.
5. Constant fatigue. Needs solitude to recharge.
6. Drawn to healing, holistic therapies, and the metaphysical.
7. Creative, artistic, imaginative.
8. Loves nature and animals.
9. Abhors clutter, chaos. Very organized.
10. Intolerant of narcissism.
11. Likes adventure, travel, seeing new things.
12. Excellent listener.
13. Watching violence, cruelty or tragedy on TV or movies is unbearable.
14. Has a calming effect on others.

Intuitive (psychic)

1. Sensitive to noise, taste, smells, colors, touch.
2. Over stimulated in crowds or noisy locations.
3. Sensitive to electrical equipment (light bulbs

may flicker when near; shock easily when touching metal).

4. Feels others emotions as if their own; cry easily.

5. Allergies and upper respiratory problems common.

6. Easily senses negativity from people, rooms, buildings, and choose to stay away.

7. Dislikes conflict. Feels inclined to resolve it.

8. A strong sense of justice and fairness.

9. Seems to read family or friend's mind. Ability to sense what others want before they ask.

10. Seems to know when someone is ill.

11. Senses the energy in a room. Sees auras.

12. Vivid dreams, especially of flying. Premonition dreams. Visits with the deceased.

13. Animals and young children want to be near you and follow you.

14. Excellent sense of direction.

Is there a scientific explanation as to why redheads experience a heightened intuition and awareness? Many scientists pass off redhead claims of these skills as <u>pseudoscience</u> - beliefs and claims that do not meet the criteria of experimentation, replication of results, nor peer reviews. In the same breath (on paper) the scientists do concede that hair is an extension of the nervous system. Hair is a sensory organ for all humans and animals.

Red hair contains more iron than other colors thus acting as a transmitter or antenna of sorts to the individual's environment. Would this not enhance the individual's ability to tap the energy surrounding her or him? Does this conjure a mental picture of a television antenna sprouting from our red heads? Geez, maybe my dad was right. We redheads really are mutant aliens?!

Actor Ray Walston starred in the
My Favorite Martian tv show.
1963

Redheads emit magical flakes of unicorn dust to make the world a better place.

Chapter 7
The Golden Crown

Redheads are a rare blend of awesomeness.

A big change for most redheads occurs in the teen years. The bullying, teasing, and name calling seems to stop. Compliments, recognition, adoration, infatuation, even a bit of jealousy become apparent. Such was the case for this redhead.

I slammed my locker door shut before any other text books could escape and clunk me on the head, then rushed off to my English class. One of my classmates rushed to catch me, "Hey Claud, wait up will ya!" Out of breath, she announced that her speech teacher wanted to see me. I did not take speech class and figured he was going to try and get me to join the debate team. "It's important," she said, then rushed off.

That was another life changing day for this redhead. Both the speech teacher and my chemistry teacher showed me a newspaper clipping announcing the return of minor league baseball to our city. The team was called the Modesto Reds. The newspaper headline read:

"Reds Seek Four Red-Headed Bat Girls."
Both teachers encouraged me to apply. I read the article detailing the idea, thought it might be an interesting job and assured both teachers I would check into it. After school, I called the number listed in the article and an appointment for an interview was set. I was to wear a pair of shorts and a T-shirt. I confirmed that I was a natural redhead. My stark white legs would probably blind the interviewer, but what the heck - if they wanted redheads, they should be aware that we don't have bronze tans.

I must admit, I had never been inter-viewed for a real job, nor had I held a job other than babysitting neighborhood kids. I had no idea what to expect. My mom told me to just smile and answer the questions truthfully. I did not know much about baseball in general, rules in particular, so hopefully that would not be a problem during the interview. If so, I'd just make something up.

The interviewer was the general manager for the minor league ball club. He was to interview and hire four redheads (real reds, not bottled), two would actually work on the field as "bat boys," the other two would work in the ticket, grandstand, and concession areas. We were to work at all home

The Golden Crown

games for the entire season, and be available for publicity photos and interviews to promote the team and its return to the city. It was a minimum wage paying job with the following perks: uniform type outfits and shoes provided by local high-end store sponsors; hair done weekly prior to home games by a local exclusive salon sponsor. Wow! So far, so good. Sounded intriguing.

The interview questioning began:

Do you play baseball? *Girls have to play softball in high school.*

What position do you play? *Mostly, left out.*

Oh, you mean left field? *No, left out on the bench - I'm a terrible player.*

Can you hit the ball? *It's hard when you're sitting on the bench.* I smiled real big and he burst out laughing.

Okay, well in baseball, how many innings in a regular game? *Thirteen.*

How many players are on a team? *Thirteen.*

Well, I mean how many players are on the field at one time? *Thirteen.* I thought he was trying to trick me with these questions.

What does the pitcher do? *He throws the ball at the batter.*

What does the umpire do? *He watches over the game and calls outs and safes.*
How many outs in an inning? *Five!*

    I smiled politely with each question and answer, gave good eye contact, and knew this job was mine, all mine. I gave strong, confident and convincing answers, but they were all completely WRONG! Despite that, I was hired on the spot! The manager told me I would have to do some serious homework to learn the rules of baseball. I asked why he had hired me if I had given all the wrong answers. He said, "Because you were so convincing and confident and you made me laugh. Oh, and your hair is gorgeous. You will be perfect for all the publicity photos and interviews."

1966 Modesto Reds Bat Girl.

    To summarize an entire baseball season as one of the redheaded bat girls: I was interviewed on local TV and radio, made special appearances and spoke at local service clubs, visited the local hospital children's ward, appeared at the away games, as well as my regular job at home games as the home team bat girl. I was also chosen to fly to New York and appear on the

TV show, *What's My Line*. The celebrity panel failed to guess my "Line" and I won $50!

The team that year included future Baseball Hall of Fame Inductees Reggie Jackson, Rollie Fingers, and Tony La Russa, as well as baseball greats Joe Rudi, Dave Duncan, Skip Lockwood, and others.

Bat Girl on the job!

I retained my bat girl position for the 1967 season with a new team and same great perks! All that for having rusty red hair! What a deal.

(Author's note: The recorded episode of the TV show can be found on YouTube: What's My Line? - Joey Bishop; PANEL: Phyllis Newman, Buddy Hackett (Sep 4, 1966).

(Author's sales pitch - the entire story of this amazing job adventure can be found in my book, "Summer on the Diamond as the 1966 Modesto Reds Bat Girl." *Available for order on Amazon or Barnes & Noble. If you like baseball, you will enjoy this book!)*

Everyone remembers the girl with red hair.

Red hair is the rarest natural color in humans. We discussed earlier how the mutation of chromosome #16 has blessed us with the MC1R gene. Now let's take a closer look at the hair itself.

The average human has about 100,000 hair follicles on his/her head. Each follicle can grow about twenty individual hairs in a person's lifetime; that would calculate out to about two million hair strands per lifetime. Is my math correct? That's a lot of hair! But wait, we also normally lose about 100-125 strands a day, so it all works out - I guess. The average growth rate for hair is .04 cm per day.

Blondes (real, not bottled) have an average of 150,000 hair follicles on their heads. Black or brown haired folks have an average of 100,000-110,000. Redheads only have an average of 90,000. WHAT? That can't be right. Are looks deceiving? Yes they are!

It is my red hair that interferes with my good sense.
All that color so close to my brain,
it plum disorients me most days.

Redheads have less hair follicles but much thicker hair strands giving the appearance of more hair. That explains why I had to have my rusty locks thinned every six weeks so my mother could get the brush through it!

As we redheaded humans age, so does our hair. Around the age of forty, our hair follicles begin thinning and become fine to the touch. We also lose more hair daily, especially at the crown. Growth slows. Those losses are not replaced, thus receding hair lines and widening part lines become more apparent. Sadly. Hysterically.

<u>Melanin</u> <u>production</u> (which gives us our hair color) also decreases, resulting in the beginning of color fade. At this point, most non-red folks begin finding gray hairs here and there, especially around the face. Men usually begin finding gray hair earlier (premature graying) then women due to genetics, stress, poor dietary, and lifestyle habits, sleep patterns, or illness.

We can't all be redheads.
There has to be someone left to envy us.

Redheads, men as well as women, do not gray. As the melanin production decreases, the red hair begins to fade to lighter shades; from a rusty red to a lighter rust, to a strawberry blondish, to a lighter blondish, to an eventual snow white.

White hair is colorless hair. The term for the result of this process is <u>achromotrichia,</u> the absence of pigment (color) in the hair.

Color fade, not necessarily related to aging, can be hastened by frequent and/or prolonged exposure to the sun. Think of it as a sunburn on the hair strands. The sun's UV rays react to the natural lipids which give hair its shine. Exposure leaves the hair looking dull, from the loss of lipids, and faded from the sun bleaching. Those harsh sun rays can also find their way to the scalp and cause a miserable sunburn. Wear a hat to protect hair and scalp from the sun!

Redheads can have multiple shades of red.
When people ask who does your highlights,
just answer, "God."

Another process in hair aging involves loss of the protein, <u>keratin</u>. Hair is made of keratin. The hair strand becomes weaker and less elastic which causes damage and breakage. It also effects the texture of the hair. Curly, wavy hair may begin to straighten, or straight hair may begin springing curls.

If redheads dislike their ginger tresses, why don't they just buy a box of Clairol or L'Oreal and dye it? Because of the curse of MC1R. The red pigment is much more firm on the hair strand than other natural colors. The strands won't take the dye without a fight. Going to a darker shade, such as a darker brown or brunette color of dye would take hold, but most likely not last very long.

To dye a rusty red color to a lighter blonde calls for harsh measures. The pigment must first be stripped with a bleach solution before attempting a lighter dye. This damages the hair and can even cause hair loss. If you want to be a blonde, just wait for the aging process! It will come soon enough.

There are people with red hair and then there are _real_ redheads.

Likewise, red hair does not like to be permed. That stubborn pigment will also shun the chemical perming solution. The keratin in red hair has up to twice as much sulphur than a blonde or brunette which makes it more difficult to absorb the perming solution. The curls and waves may set for awhile before gradually loosening and a repeated treatment is needed. Frequent perming also damages the hair and can cause hair loss.

At this point, with all this red hair knowledge, you should begin to understand why redheads are so temperamental. It has to be due to the stubborn pigment on the hair strands. With thousands of stubborn hair strands, it stands to reason, redheads would have stubborn, temperamental personalities! I wonder if any scientific studies would confirm this theory?

Our glorious golden crowns do not have diamonds or pearls, instead we have sulphur and iron with a touch of gold.

Chapter 8

Sun Dots

A redhead without freckles
is like a night without stars.

No one is born with freckles, not even redheads. They first appear in children from ages two to three as they are exposed to sunlight. Have you ever seen a redhead without freckles? Not very likely, very rare indeed. So what happens? Where do those little spots come from?

My family lived in Seattle, Washington for several years. I tell people my freckles are actually rust spots due to living in the cloudy, rainy climate. Other redheads claim their freckles are sun kisses, angel kisses, red cinnamon spice, sun spots, sun dots, sun germs... the list is endless. One redhead told me he was standing in front of a big fan when the proverbial sh#t hit it and splattered his face! Yuck!

Freckles are a redhead's glitter.

Freckles are actually a result of genetics and sun exposure. With a quick glance at a face full of freckles, they all seem to be shades of round brown spots. Closer examination with a magnifying glass will find no two freckles are exactly alike on the person nor are they the same shape or size on any other person, not even on an identical twin or close family member. You might say, freckles are like brown snowflakes! No two are ever the same.

Even the term, freckle, is unusual. The Middle English word freken came from old Norse freknur meaning freckled. The Greek word and medical term used today for freckles is ephelides.

Ephelides (freckles) are flat, brown, circular shaped spots 1-2mm in size or about the size of a pin head. The color tones are usually uniform ranging from dark reddish brown to a darkish beige or light tan in relation to the skin tone and hair color. The darker the hair, the darker the freckle tone; the lighter the hair, the lighter the freckle tone. These freckles fade in winter and return to their previous color when exposed to sunlight in spring and summer.

Lentigines or lentigo is the medical term for freckles larger in size and darker than ephelides. The term is from Latin meaning lentil, like the legume. These pigmented freckle spots can easily be found at the site of previous sun burns especially where excessive sun damage occurred.

These lentigines do not fade in the winter, nor do they darken in the summer.

Liver spots are lentigines specifically found on the back of our hands. The name may be related to the darker brownish color of the liver; however, they have nothing to do with the liver itself. Many wrongly assume the spots are a result or a sign of old age. The spots are only an indication of excessive sun damage on the back of the hands. They do not fade in winter nor do they darken in summer.

Freckles are most commonly spotted on the face; however, any skin surface exposed to UVB radiation (sunlight) will stimulate the formation of freckles. Contrary to misguided belief and/or ridicule, freckles are not a skin disease, but a condition of genetics. That pesky MC1R gene, which gives us our hair color, also controls the color of our skin and freckles via melanin. Melanin is the pigment (color) found in the skin, hair, and iris of the eye. There are three types of melanin: eumelanin (the most common), and pheomelanin (these two melanins were discussed briefly in an earlier chapter), along with neuromelanin, which is found in the brain - we aren't studying the brain today.

Higher levels of eumelanin are found in folks with darker hair and skin while those with more pheomelanin will have fair skin with red or blonde hair. Those of us blessed with the MC1R gene have an imbalance of eumelanin and pheomelanin. That imbalance is what causes the various shades of redhead hair colors. Melanin pigments are produced in cells called melanocytes which control that balance.

When exposed to the harmful UVB sunlight, the melanocytes are triggered to increase production of melanin; this process is called photoprotection. Melanin will jump into protection mode to reflect and absorb the sun rays protecting the skin from the harmful sunlight.

At this point in photoprotection, the darker skinned folks with the eumelanin will have a lovely, even, bronze suntan. The fair complected will have the lesser pheomelanin melanocytes clumping together to try and protect the skin with a bronze tan, but instead, they get a gazillion bronze spots! One might surmise the gazillion spots would eventually/hopefully smoosh together across the skin surface giving the pale redhead a beautiful golden tan. (This author has been waiting many loooong years for the smoosh effect to occur - it hasn't happened.)

Freckles have very little potential for malignancy. They will fade with less sun exposure in the winter and darken in the summer. Freckles will also fade with the aging process, just like the hair.

Freckles are like sweet seasoning for your face. Cinnamon and sugar.

Now, back to the eumelanin and pheomelanin imbalance. Think of this imbalance as two genetic siblings fighting over color! One kid wants the eumelanin for darker hair and a bronzy tan. The other kid loves the red hair but doesn't really care about the bronzy tan and likes his gazillion brown freckles; he wants more pheomelanin. But wait! Along comes the neighbor kid with even more pheomelanin to join the fight. That kid has such blonde hair, it almost looks white and his freckles look anemic. The blondie neighbor kid with the highest levels of pheomelanin wins the genetic disturbance of color imbalance! In more scientific terms: the more pheomelanin the lighter the red hair. AND the lighter the freckles. AND the lighter the eye color! All because of the MC1R and its mysteries. The gene is present, but there are a variety of different elements or levels of color in every individual. If you have four MC1R present siblings, they can all have different colors of hair, from a dark auburn red to a white blonde. Their freckles will also vary in color - darker to lighter. Just like my siblings!

BEWARE!
Freckles give redheads superpowers!

Moles and birthmarks are not freckles. Moles are usually darker in appearance and slightly raised from the skin surface. Some moles may even have hair growing from their center. They are not caused by the sun and may fade with aging. Moles that become larger, more raised, itchy, or bleed must be examined by a physician to rule out a potential malignant melanoma (skin cancer).

All fair-skinned folks should know the ABCDE's to watch for in determining a malignant melanoma:

A - <u>Asymmetry</u>. Be suspicious of moles that are asymmetric, i.e. if you cannot draw a line down the middle of the mole and match up both sides it is asymmetrical.

B - <u>Borders</u>. Be suspicious of moles with fuzzy or ill-defined borders.

C - <u>Color</u>. Be suspicious of moles with variegated color throughout or two toned.

D - <u>Diameter</u>. Be suspicious of larger moles, greater than 6 mm in diameter (a bit less then 1/4 inch).

E - <u>Evolving</u>. Be suspicious of moles that are changing in color, texture, size.

Birthmarks are abnormalities of the skin present at birth or within four to six weeks thereafter. There are a variety of names for the marks, usually dependent on the color: cafe au lait (dark shades of brown), hemangioma (pink or red), nevus (brown), strawberry (pink or red). There are also the folklore names for birthmarks: angel kisses (the pink or red lipstick mark left by the kiss of an angel prior to birth) and stork bites (the red or blue bite mark left by the stork as it held the infant by the back of the neck for delivery).

Any of these skin coloration marks are most pronounced on a fair skinned infant at birth. The marks are usually odd shaped with colors ranging from pale pink to dark red, light to dark brown. The mark is flat to the skin surface, and may fade with age. They commonly appear on the face, scalp, back of the neck, chest, or back. The marks are usually vascular in nature, made up of blood vessels that had not yet formed correctly before birth. The clinical term for birthmarks is <u>congenital melanocytic naevi,</u> but "birthmarks" are much easier to remember and pronounce!

Freckles are sun kisses in the daylight
and skin stars at night.

Chapter 9

Rare & Radiant

Redheads are not fragile like a flower,
we are fragile like a bomb.

In the mid-1950s, my grandparents had a huge swimming pool built in their backyard. We kids watched the construction from day one and counted the days until we could jump in. From a six-year-old's perspective, it seemed to take forever to build. When it was finally finished, the workers connected a long fire hose to the nearby fire hydrant and filled the pool. We anxiously waited on the patio clad in our bathing suits and wrapped in our beach towels. It took several hours, but we stood by watching as the water level crept higher and higher. FINALLY, the pool was filled to the brim with fresh clean, freezing cold water! We jumped in as soon as we were allowed, then jumped right back out! Toooo cold. Luckily there was a built-in heater, but it took several days to warm the thousands of gallons of ice cold water. We tested the water everyday until it met with our high standards for perfect conditions, then jumped in, played, and swam with abandon for hours on end.

Thus began many summers of fun swimming all day long and paying for it with the worst sunburns you could ever imagine. Coppertone suntan lotion was fairly new to the market at that time. My mom bought bags full of the brown plastic bottles and nearly drowned me in it. My siblings didn't burn, they tanned; the Coppertone worked for them. I burned, blistered, peeled - repeatedly. The Coppertone "suntan" failed me.

Iconic Coppertone ad.

My mother was exasperated with my sunburns and the whining that went along with them. She wiped my burnt, blistered shoulders and back with white vinegar to "take the sting out," she said, then slathered half a jar of Noxzema on my face, arms, shoulders, and back. The cool white Noxzema felt wonderful and I swear I could hear my skin sizzle when it was applied.

Noxzema! Sunburn savior!

To keep me out of the sun, she threatened to keep me from the pool altogether or only let me swim after the sun set. I voiced my displeasure at both ideas. Finally, she found zinc oxide paste and spread it all over my face then made me wear one of Dad's white t-shirts over my bathing suit. I looked like a freak, but at least I could go swimming. The sun's rays did not penetrate the zinc oxide paste and were only slightly deterred by the t-shirt.

With the burn came the peel after several days. My sister loved to pull the peeling skin off my back and arms to see how big a pile she could make with it. The little piles were usually more than a handful. She had a contest with herself to see if she could pull the longest piece without it tearing. Awww, the burning memories. Now the scars.

Redheads do not tan!
They have only two skin color settings:
pure ghostly white or cooked lobster red.

Let's explore sunburn for a bit.

Redheads are known for their pale, fair skin caused by lower levels of eumelanin and higher levels of pheomelanin. As mentioned in the previous chapter on freckle formation, redheads do not have the protection from harmful UV sun rays those with darker hair and skin have. A few minutes in the noonday sun, especially near water, results in a brilliant red sun BURN, not a lovely bronze TAN.

*Redheads can get a sunburn
from the light in the refrigerator.*

Obviously, sunburn is caused from too much exposure to the sun, specifically the overexposure to ultraviolet (UV) radiation. The scientific explanation is that sunburn is caused by an inflammatory response in the tissue triggered by direct DNA damage from UV radiation. Any way you describe the cause, the sun is the culprit. The sun gives off three wavelengths or rays of ultraviolet radiation (light): UVA, UVB, and UVC; luckily UVC does not reach the Earth's surface. UVA rays bombard us no matter what the season or weather. The sky may be crystal clear, overcast clouds, or stormy. You may be wearing light weight clothing or sitting near tint-free window glass - the UVA rays are present and will find you and your delicate fair skin.

UVA rays penetrate deep into the skin layers damaging skin cells and altering DNA as it goes. This initiates multiple protective chemical reactions too complicated and lengthy to discuss here. Needless to say, those reactions will be noticeable ten or twenty years later as your skin becomes leathery and wrinkled; that old age weathered, outdoorsy look.

UVB rays are a bit lazier, but nonetheless dangerous, even deadly. These rays are strongest in the summer especially between 10 AM and 4 PM, depending on your geographical location. They are sneaky and can reflect off light colored buildings, concrete, water, or snow during the winter months. UVA rays contribute to cancer, but UVB rays often cause cancer.

Artificial UV exposure will also cause burns. The most common artificial exposure can be found in tanning beds. UV exposure from welding arcs and ultraviolet germicidal irradiation will also damage the skin with burns.

Sunburn? It's just my skin trying to match my hair.

Sunburns increase the risk of skin cancers. The risk increases with the cumulative number of sunburns in a lifetime. There are three main types of skin cancer: melanoma, basal-cell carcinoma, and squamous-cell carcinoma. All can be deadly.

The eyes can also suffer damage from sun exposure. Sunburn of the cornea is common in winter sports such as skiing as well as summer sports on or near water. Cumulative eye burns will lead to the development of age-related macular degeneration and cataracts. In some cases, a concentration of melanin (freckles) may form within the iris (the colored part) of the eye. Look at yourself in a mirror, close up, and check the colored part of your eye. Are there tiny little brown freckles there? Dust off those sun glasses and wear them when you are outside in the sunlight. Your old age vision will thank you for caring enough when you were younger.

Sunburn on fair skinned folks can occur within less than fifteen minutes of sun exposure. That initial burn may not become visible for another thirty to sixty minutes while uninterrupted exposure to the sun continues further burning. Peak redness will appear within twelve to twenty-four hours. Within six hours after exposure, the sunburn pain becomes increasingly uncomfortable as the burn continues destroying the deeper skin tissue/cells for up to seventy-two hours. The longer the sun exposure, the deeper and more severe the damage becomes. Tiny blisters may begin to form on the burned skin surface with the intensity of pain also increasing substantially.

Besides being uncomfortable and suffering burn site pain, a severe burn can cause swelling to the area, flu-like symptoms, fever, chills, nausea, headache, and extreme fatigue. These symptoms are a result of the immune system shifting into overdrive trying to repair the damage to the skin and underlying tissue.

After a few days, the skin becomes very itchy and begins to peel. The immune system has done its job and is now sloughing off the dead cells as fresh new skin is forming under the damaged outer layer. Another sunburn at this stage, on top of the fresh new skin, will be detrimental to your future in retaining beautiful cancer free, healthy skin.

The most commonsensical way to avoid these sun problems would be to:

1. Stay out of the sun (nearly impossible for some).

Never Let A Ginger SNAP

2. Apply sunscreen liberally as directed by the brand.

Back in the 1950s, the term most commonly used was "suntan lotion." The ideology and other factors soon changed. Now the term is "sunscreen." There are hundreds of different brands with a variety of SPF numbers. Sun Protection Factor refers to the measure of how well the product will protect you from UVB rays. SPF 30 is most commonly used for all skin types. When applied correctly it will be fully effective for two hours blocking 97% of UVB rays. SPF 50, often advertised for facial application and for children, will also be effective for two hours, but will block 98% of UVB rays.

At least thirty minutes prior to sun exposure, the sunscreen should be applied and allowed to soak into the skin. For best results preventing sunburn, reapply every two hours or more often when sweating heavily or swimming. Don't forget those UV rays will find you even on a cloudy day; lather up! For redheads especially, even with multiple and frequent layers of sunscreen along with protective clothing, those rays will find the tiniest piece of unprotected skin and add a lobster like coloration to form another gazillion freckles causing damage that will last into the future.

It's a redhead thing - laying outside in the sun for just 20 minutes and catching on fire.

Redheads are known for their sensitive skin and glowing fire engine red coloring after a bit of sun exposure. Some redheads are actually allergic to the sun and avoid exposure at all costs. Just a few minutes in the sun might result in a fine red rash at the exposure site(s), or large itchy hives all over the body, or feeling ill, as if having the flu.

Allergic reactions to the chemicals in various sunscreens are also common in redheads, causing rashes, swelling, nausea and an overall ill feeling. Extreme sun sensitivity, especially in the fair skinned, can be an early sign of lupus; an inflammatory disease caused when the body's immune system attacks its own tissues.

Did you know, skin is the largest organ of the human body? Yes! Skin is an organ, an external organ at that. All our other organs are inside, under seven layers of skin tissue. The skin alone of an average size adult weighs about eight pounds.

Stretched out in a line, it would measure 20-22 feet long.

The skin's job is to protect everything under it; the muscles, bones, nerves, blood vessels, and all the internal organs. The skin is our body's security system, an insulating shield, protecting us from germs, bacteria, viruses, along with the elements in our environment; extreme temperatures, harmful chemicals, and damaging sunlight. The skin is waterproof. It also protects us from excessive water loss, regulates our body temperature, and is the only organ that permits touch and the direct application of cold or heat. When severely damaged, the miraculous skin will try to heal itself by forming scar tissue, thus continuing to protect the underlying systems.

Ayurvedic medicine has been around for the past 3,000 years. The practitioners believed individuals with red hair who were prone to frustration, anger, arrogance, impatience, and general feelings of ill health (sounds like all of us?) released the toxins of these feelings through their skin. The toxins caused skin conditions of eczema and dermatitis as well as an increase in hay fever and allergies. Might this ancient knowledge be a viable theory today?

Perhaps the most amazing thing redheads and their skin are known for is the ability to synthesize vitamin D. Recall back in Chapter 3 how the evolution of the genetic drift enabled the light skinned folks to synthesize and store vitamin D longer in order to protect their bone strength in the Northern climates. How does that work?

The best way to explain this is simply to call it the redhead's skin magic! The scientific explanation is a bit more involved, even complicated, but here is a layman's interpretation: Vitamin D, collectively, is a group of fat-soluble secosteroids. The most important in the group is cholecalciferol, aka vitamin D3. Here is where the skin magic happens! A chemical reaction occurs deep within the lower layers of the skin when the outer layer of a fair skinned redhead is exposed to UVB sunlight. The cholecalciferol is produced in those layers, picked up and sent to the liver. The liver magically converts it to calcifediol and throws it off to the kidneys to form calcitriol. This end product now acts like a hormone circulating in the blood stream to regulate and store concentrations of calcium and phosphate. Those two elements are crucial for strong bones and teeth as well as cellular growth, neuromuscular, immune functions, and assisting in the reduction of inflammation.

With the increased use of sunscreen, the medical and scientific communities now notice more individuals with symptoms of vitamin D deficiency, primarily in the fair skinned folks. The most common complaint is severe low back pain and generalized bone pain especially in the legs and joints. Young children with vitamin D deficiency can develop rickets; a softening and weakening of their bones. Other symptoms may be depression, frequent colds, flu, and infections, overwhelming fatigue and tiredness, muscle pain, sometimes hair loss, and slow healing wounds; all symptoms of an immune system function on the fritz.

Bone loss is easily attributed to low calcium levels; however, low vitamin D and calcium work together along with phosphate to keep the bones strong. Without that elemental camaraderie there is no bone strength and serious problems manifest. Obviously, that is what happened those thousands of years ago when our ancestors were "drifting" - until their bodies adapted, their bones failed them, teeth fell out, they could not heal from wounds, they succumbed to diseases… Maybe they became mushy treats for dinosaurs and other predators?

Vitamin D supplements are recommended for low laboratory levels and symptoms of deficiency. Today, in the United States and other countries, vitamin D is added to milk, breakfast cereals, and orange juice. Food sources of vitamin D include fatty fish (salmon, sardines, herring), canned tuna, egg yolks, and mushrooms.

So if anyone asks you how redheads can synthesize vitamin D so well, just tell them "it's their skin magic."

A day without a redhead
is like a day without sunshine.

Chapter 10
Medical Mysteries & Marvels

Hell hath no greater fury
then a redhead in a dental chair.

In the 1950s there were no fancy pediatric dentists in my hometown nor any town. No cute Disney pictures lining the walls, no video monitor on the ceiling showing Disney movies or animal nature videos, and no smiley, cheerful assistants in bright colored uniforms to take your mind off the torture the mean old dentist would be inflicting on you.

My first redhead experience with going to the dentist at age six or seven was tragic. It was tragic for my mother, the office staff, and the dentist himself. His office was in the same multi-story building as my grandfather's insurance office. As you entered the main lobby of the building, there was a huge aquarium filled with unusual fish swimming slowly in the murky water. It was located in front of the two elevators to distract visitors while they waited for the slow cars to return to the lobby. My mom tricked me that eventful day by telling me we were going to see Grandpa, but first we had to go see Dr. Dentist. I had no clue who or what Dr. Dentist was. I soon found out.

First I had to climb onto Dr. Dentist's weird chair. The little room it was in had lots of strange gadgets, an odd overhead light, a window that faced a red brick building, and an unusual smell. This old guy with white fuzzy hair surrounding a bald head and coke-bottle-bottom eyeglasses came into the room, told me to open my mouth and started poking around at my teeth. He told me I had several holes in my teeth called cavities because I ate too much candy, and didn't brush my teeth very well. He said he could tell what I had for breakfast just by looking at my teeth: bacon, scrambled eggs, toast with red jam. I was aghast! He was a damn LIAR! I had a bowl of oatmeal for breakfast! There was no immediate bond of trust formed there. I knew then he must be incompetent. Unfortunately, his other observations were correct. I was, and still am, a carboholic - candy, cookies, ice cream, cake, cupcakes, basically anything with lots of sugar.

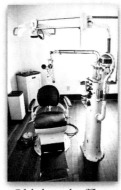
Old dental office equipment.

Never Let A Ginger SNAP

Then that old coot said he was going to fix my cavities. All I had to do was sit quietly while he made some buzzing noises in my mouth. But first he would give me some medicine to make my mouth go to sleep. "Now, close your eyes real tight while I give your mouth the medicine," he said. The details of that ordeal were worse than the most horrific nightmare you could ever have. The following terms come to mind (create your own images): frightful, hellish, godawful, barbaric, cruel, vicious, excruciating, traumatic, torturous… AND that was just for the injection of novocaine! His version of "some buzzing in my mouth" was more like a jackhammer tearing up the street corner. Repeat all of the above horrific terms more forcefully.

Author's vision of the old coot dentist!

Like any true redhead, I fought back! I kicked, I bit, I slapped, and I screamed bloody murder. My mother was called in to calm me down. She threatened me with parental violence (the belt or the wooden spoon upon arrival at home or the hairbrush now; she kept it in her purse), loss of

Medical Mysteries & Marvels

swimming privileges, and loss of bike riding for a week. I was not fazed by her threats. Then she restrained my hands, and sat on my legs. I knew I was being tortured and probably murdered. My mouth never went to sleep and whatever that buzzing was, hurt like a .... (fill in the blank with the worst pain you've ever experienced as a child or an adult and sprinkle it with a variety of adult cuss words).

When the ordeal was over, Dr. Dentist told my mother we were not welcome to return as he tended to his bloody bite injuries. Thank goodness. There were more cavities that needed attention according to Dr. Fuzzy Headed Dentist. So mother found another dentist, bless her cruel heart. Repeat all of the above through two more unfortunate dental professionals. They just didn't seem to understand the mouth numbing medicine did not work on me and that buzzing thing was going to kill me. So I was labeled an uncooperative brat, a wimp, a fake, and invited never to return. I also lost swimming privileges, bike riding for fun (still could ride to school of course), got the hairbrush across the butt multiple times, and no candy. Damnit. Double damnit. I surely suffered sugar withdrawal symptoms.

Never Let A Ginger SNAP

On the fourth try, Mother found a new dentist just starting his practice. Obviously, word in the dental community had not yet reached him about the little redhead that punched, bit, and kicked. She warned him ahead of time about my previous bad experiences. He said he would try something different. But I was going to try something different, too! When we arrived in the parking area, Mother got out of the car while I pretended to tie my shoe, but locked the car doors instead! I thought I was a genius until she stuck the key in the door lock to unlock the dang door then dragged me by the hair and arm into the office yelping all the way.

Once inside, this Dr. Dentist sat quietly with me before immediately pouncing into my mouth. He was young and very handsome, fresh out of dental school. He showed me all his dental tools and explained what they did. That buzzing thing was actually called a drill. He showed me how to brush my teeth using a model of teeth, then asked if I wanted to play a game. He had me chew a strawberry flavored tablet

Author's vision of the young handsome dentist!

that would turn my teeth red then handed me a mirror to look at them. "Now brush your teeth like you would at home," he directed. There was still red in multiple spots so he showed me how to move the toothbrush to clear the spots. Then he gave me a couple of nice new colored toothbrushes to take home.

Next, he told me about cavities and how he had to fix them or my teeth would start to hurt so bad I wouldn't be able to eat sweets anymore. THAT got my attention - no more candy? I told him the mouth medicine did not make my mouth go to sleep and how it always hurt so bad to fix the cavities with that buzzing drill. We made a deal. He would give me some "magic medicine that will make you laugh and not be scared" then he would give me the mouth medicine. He said if my teeth started to hurt, just raise my hand and he would fix it. Hallelujah, someone was finally listening to me!

The magic medicine was nitrous oxide, aka laughing gas. About ten minutes after receiving the novocaine, I raised my hand while he was drilling away. He immediately stopped and gave me more novocaine. This went on for three more injections, each about ten minutes apart. He was true to his word as I was to mine; no kicking, no biting, no screaming. I was in love with him because he listened to me and he was also very handsome. I thanked him for not hurting me and told him I would let my mother bring me back anytime. I also got to pick a toy out of his toy chest for excellent behavior! I thought my mother was going to faint when I found her in the waiting room and showed her my Certificate for Excellent Behavior, my new toy, and two new toothbrushes. A day to remember.

Many, many years later while having my first knee surgery, I scared the living daylights out of the entire operating room crew, the orthopedist, and the anesthetist. I had been given spinal anesthesia so I was completely numb from the waist down. I was also given something to relax me and I was out like a light - for a very short period of time. I roused a bit and heard the crew talking quietly then I heard loud pounding. The orthopedic doctor was pounding the staple into my lower leg bone. I did not feel any pain, just pressure on my leg. I let out a blood curdling scream because my brain told me that pounding should hurt! Total chaos ensued. A metal tray with instruments loudly clattered to the tile floor, dropped by a startled nurse. The orthopedic doctor yelled at the anesthesiologist, "She's awake? Knock her out!" at the same time the anesthesiologist yelled out, "Jesus C#&@!T, what the hell?" One of the nurses called to me, "Claudia, can you feel that?" I said, "No, but I thought it would probably hurt if I could feel it so I thought you all should know." I heard a few chuckles before my lights went out.

This story spread like wildfire through the hospital (no HIPPA laws back then) since I was the head nurse of the Coronary Care Unit at that time. When I was fully awake and resting in my room, the two doctors and the head nurse from the Operating Room paid me a collective visit. They had come to tell me how I had given them all a heart attack and soiled their underwear when I screamed! They had never had a patient wake up in the middle of a surgery. I apologized profusely and reminded them, things never seem to go right, medically, with redheads. I was proof.

Two other surgical procedures with anesthesia nightmares involving a redhead occurred when my grandson and granddaughter were born. An epidural was given to the laboring redhead mom-to-be when the contractions became unbearable, but only one side of her body became numb. The doctor was notified and was completely puzzled as to how that could be. The soon-to-be father told the doctor he would only pay for half the epidural! The laboring mom-to-be and the puzzled doctor failed to see the humor at that time; I thought it was appropriate and giggled. A bit later, with the one side still numb, an emergency cesarean section had to be performed for the early arrival of a perfect red haired boy.

A couple of years later, the second baby demanded she arrive early (surely another redhead taking control?). Another emergency cesarean section had to be done with a spinal for anesthesia. Mom-to-be was awake and both sides numb from the spinal - for a few minutes. After the perfect little red haired girl was born, the obstetrician began putting things back together and suturing. The mom was suddenly no longer numb and felt everything. The pain and pressure was extremely intense, beyond excruciating. Can you even imagine? She cried out to the doctor, "I can feel what you're doing! Stop!" The doctor told the anesthesiologist, "Do something!" The next thing the new mom remembers was waking in the recovery room all put back together and seeing her feisty little red haired baby girl.

There are thousands of stories worldwide about redheads, mostly women, waking up during a surgical procedure. There is even a name for it: anesthesia awareness. Many experienced excruciating pain, many were paralyzed by the anesthesia and could not talk or move, many could hear the conversations, but could not respond due to the intubation tube. Real life redhead nightmares for sure. Seem to be quite common.

Other reports come from redheads waking in the recovery room noting anesthesia reactions of uncontrollable severe shaking with teeth jarring shivers. Warm blankets have no effect. Small amounts of intravenous Meperedine (narcotic Demerol) stop the tremors within seconds. But why are these medical and dental occurrences common in redheads? Or is this a myth?

Multiple small studies by a variety of interested groups began in 2000 with the goal of determining the connection, if any, between redheads and their reactions to pain. Different groups found their results conflicted with other groups' results so further studies were not actively pursued. That did not stop dentists and anesthesiologists from frequently talking among themselves about, "...that one patient I had with red hair..." The topic usually concerned the amount of medication needed for pain control which most often exceeded normal dosage limits. All seemed to agree redheads were difficult to anesthetize for dental or surgical procedures; however, nothing concrete had yet been established as to why. It appeared these observations would continue to simply be passed off as urban legends until Dr. Daniel Sessler, an anesthesiologist at the Cleveland Clinic in Cleveland, Ohio, and his colleagues at the University of Louisville in Louisville, Kentucky decided to conduct a more intensive investigation.

Dr. Daniel Sessler.

"The persistent rumor in the anesthesia community was that redheads were difficult to anesthetize," said Dr. Sessler. "They didn't go under, had a lot of pain, and didn't respond well to anesthesia. Urban legends usually don't start studies, but it was such an intriguing observation."

The study recruited twenty healthy Caucasian women from the Greater Louisville, Kentucky area between the ages of eighteen and forty, ten with natural red hair and ten with dark black or brown hair. Blood samples were taken from each to determine the presence or absence of an MC1R allele. Nine of the ten redheads had the gene. Of course, none of the others had it.

The volunteers were each given the same general anesthesia amount to begin with then subjected to a noxious electrical stimulation to elicit a physical response of reflexive movement in the arms or legs. When a response was recorded, the volunteer was then given incremental doses of anesthesia until the volunteer reached the point of non-movement; fully anesthetized.

The results of this research in 2004 concluded that redheads with the MC1R gene needed 20% more general anesthesia than darker haired women. "That people with the red hair phenotype require more anesthesia is not only of practical importance, but suggests that genetic characteristics contribute to differences in anesthetic requirements in humans," replied Dr.

Edwin B. Liem, one of the researchers involved with the study. It was also noted that redheads perceive and process pain differently than others. Findings from this study could help future researchers understanding of the various systems in producing unconsciousness and altering pain perception.

(Author's note: Anesthetics and analgesics have two separate actions. Anesthesia numbs the pain and other senses at the same time, i.e. lidocaine for local numbing or a variety of inhaled, systemic medications to put you to sleep for a surgical procedure. Analgesics relieve pain without numbing - over the counter pain relievers, opioids, oral narcotics.)

It was also noted the injection of novocaine/lidocaine for local anesthesia is less effective in redheads. Dr. Sessler stated, "If you give them local anesthesia, they don't get as much pain relief as other people do." The use of local anesthesia for suturing a large cut, taking a skin biopsy, or any such medical necessity for lidocaine on a redhead, has the same effect as the use of novocain or lidocaine for dental procedures. The numbing effect does not last long enough to complete the procedure. The half-life (how long the effects last)

Medical Mysteries & Marvels

of local anesthesia in the body of a non-redhead is about 1.5-2 hours. In a redhead it is 10-30 minutes.

Further study in 2005 concluded that redheads with a greater resistance to local anesthesia also experienced increased sensitivity to thermal pain, extremes of hot or cold.

More recent studies have found that although redheads are more sensitive to certain types of pain and more immune to anesthetics, their skin is tougher than others which leads them to be less susceptible to skin-related pain. Professor Lars Arendt-Nielsen arrived at that conclusion and explained, "Our tests showed that redheads are less sensitive to this particular type of pain. They react less to pressure close to the injected area, or to a pinprick. They seem to be a bit better protected, and that is a really interesting finding."

A large study undertaken in 2012 by Australian researchers followed 468 surgical patients undergoing general anesthesia. Their findings showed patients with red hair had no higher anesthesia drug requirements than patients with other hair colors. Hmmm.

Still another study, done in 2013, by the same researchers at the Cleveland Clinic found no difference in the administration of intravenous anesthetic needs of redheads compared to others. That study concluded: "Anecdotal impressions among anesthesiologists that propofol (a common intravenous anesthetic) requirements are increased in redheads thus seem unsubstantiated."

Confused? Yes! The study results are as mixed and confusing as any redhead you might know! More studies need to come, it is inevitable, and several are in the works at this time. In the meantime, do you hear us redheads screaming bloody murder in the background?

One good thing has come from all of these studies, even if they seem conflicted. It has taken many years for the dental community to see and understand that redheads feel dental pain and react differently to the effects of local anesthesia. A toothache experienced by a non-redhead is an inconvenience and a nuisance, but a toothache in a redhead is excruciating and unbearable. Some of the studies confirmed the dentists observations; unfortunately, there are still many dentists that believe this is a myth. It is likely they have few, if any, redheaded patients.

There is hope for us! The younger medical and dental school graduates seem to have an understanding that we redheads have unusual sensitivities to local anesthesia. A recent visit to a young dermatologist for skin lesion biopsies resulted in the physician instructing his nurse to "Give her extra at both sites, she's a redhead." Wow!

Does the MC1R gene mutation play a role in the effects of anesthesia and analgesics on redheads? Of course it does! The gene belongs to a family of receptors with all sorts of duties, including the duty of pain reception in the brain which, in turn, regulates the body's sensitivity to pain. The MC1R gene mutation also stimulates endorphin hormone secretion within the brain and nervous system. One of the duties of endorphins is to provide pain relief and the sense of pleasure and well being. Since the mutated gene in redheads is different than the gene in others, the difference in pain sensation and reaction to medications is also different. Perhaps unique.

Along the lines of dental and surgical procedures comes the mystery vs myth of redheads bruising and bleeding more than others. Again, we investigate the MC1R gene.

That relentless redhead gene can be found on endothelial cells, on the lining of the blood vessels, as well as on immune cells. All of these vessels and cells are involved with the blood clotting process. Endothelial cells form the barrier between vessels and tissue and control the flow of cells and fluids into and out of a tissue. The endothelium provides a surface on which blood does not clot. So, it stands to reason that redheads and their genetic mutation - the MC1R gene - should, in fact, bruise and bleed more than others.

A variety of studies conclude coagulation tests on redheads are within normal limits; no difference in clotting can be found, therefore, no substantiated reason for the abnormal bleeding claims. Some studies conclude that because the redheads have such pale skin, bruises are more visible than on darker skinned folks.

Studies also concluded post-operative hemorrhage in tonsillectomy cases between redheads and other hair colors were the same. One group of researchers had the audacity to conclude "There is no basis in fact that redheads bleed more; it is an excuse by surgeons to defend problematic bleeding in their patients they could not control." I'll bet that made all the surgeons happy.

Medical professionals agree, redheads are a challenge in a number of ways!

BUT, ask any emergency room physician, any obstetrical physician, any surgeon, any surgical nurse, recovery room nurse, any medical professional in any location, or any redhead that has experienced childbirth (natural or cesarean section), a traumatic injury, any surgical procedure, or a simple slice to a finger while preparing a meal, if redheads bleed more than others. You will be overwhelmed by the affirmative responses and personal stories about big bloody messes. Any medical professional who sees a redhead or fair-skinned patient knows to be prepared for a blood bath at one point or another. Everyone seems to notice and affirm these situations, but no studies have confirmed them - yet. More studies must be undertaken to understand exactly how the MC1R gene effects these bloody situations before the blood banks run dry when a redhead is injured.

Other medical studies involving redheads were more successful in their findings. Studies found a link between melanoma, Parkinson's disease, and endometriosis (endometriosis will be discussed later). In 1986 and 1988, 130,000 men and women participated in a study which asked their natural hair color when they were between the ages of eighteen and twenty one. The large group was divided by hair color: black, brown, blonde, and red. Data was collected for several years and studied in 2002. The conclusion was that redheads had a three times higher risk of Parkinson's disease than those with black hair. Blondes followed with one and a half times the risk, with brunettes at one and a quarter.

Years later, utilizing previous data from Parkinson's and melanoma studies (those earlier melanoma studies found redheads at three times higher risk of melanoma than others), researchers at Massachusetts General Hospital found evidence the MC1R gene linked the two: increased risk of melanoma with increased risk of Parkinson's disease. That rascal MC1R was messing with the dopamine levels in the brain by destroying the dopamine producing neurons. Loss of those neurons causes abnormal brain activity which leads to the shaky motor movement symptoms of Parkinson's disease.

One more study to disprove mystery vs myth comes from the British Journal of Cancer. The study included men with brown, black, blonde, and natural red hair. At the conclusion the results noted redheaded men were 54% less likely to develop prostate cancer than the others. What a relief to know for the redheaded men!

We didn't choose the redhead life.
The redhead life chose us.

Chapter 11
Fiery & Feisty

There is no creature as dangerous
as an angry redhead.

It was a cold, foggy December night when I saw a hot air balloon up close and personal for the first time. The pilot was giving free tether rides to promote the Grand Opening location of a new electronics store. It was the most magnificent, magical thing I'd ever seen. The balloon's silken fabric glistened and sparkled in the surrounding lights.

I waited patiently in line watching the entire operation. The balloon was eight stories tall and lit up like a giant Tiffany lamp when the pilot pulled the burner. The pilot greeted each passenger as they climbed into the wicker basket and got situated. When he pulled the burner it was very loud and scared some of the folks as the flame shot directly up into the balloon. It reminded me of a roaring, fire breathing dragon. The heat was what caused the balloon to gently lift about fifty feet into the air. Four tether lines were secured to vehicles on the ground and pulled taut as the balloon ascended.

Fiery & Feisty

I was the last in line and quickly climbed aboard for my turn. The pilot was young, handsome, and wore a flight suit with the store logo on the pocket. He pulled the toggle on the burner and we slowly lifted up. The basket, or gondola, was wicker with leather padding around the top edges. Four propane tanks stood upright in each of the four corners with tubing connecting them to the two burners. There were aircraft like instruments on a small panel with dials, sensors, and indicators.

I leaned over the edge of the basket and waved to my kids and their friends below telling the pilot they were all mine for the evening - birthday party for my oldest son. "So, why don't you just cut the ropes, let's fly away right now and take me away from all of them?" I politely asked, pointing to the group below. He laughed and said balloons don't fly at night. I started asking several hundred questions about the balloon itself, how it operates, where they are flown, sizes, shapes, piloting... He answered all my questions without hesitation. When I asked, "How can I get one of these?" he paused for a moment then replied, "Women can't fly balloons, they aren't strong enough."

As I mentioned before, he was quite handsome and he had the prettiest green eyes that sparkled when he lit the burner, but he was an IDIOT! He obviously knew I was a woman. Perhaps he didn't see my rusty red hair? NEVER, NEVER, EVER tell a redhead she can't do something! It might put your life in extreme danger. Seriously.

The author "puttin" the heat to the sheets!"
Balloon lingo: heating the balloon for inflation
followed by lift off.

It took a year to get my commercial hot air balloon pilot license, a small sporty economy model balloon (only seven stories high with a smaller gondola), and a business plan to run my own commercial ride company on my days off

Fiery & Feisty

Our Wayward Wind.

from the hospital. In the first flight competition I entered, I won first place. That same week I was one of only two women pilots competing in a larger event with forty other balloonists. I placed in the top ten. And, guess who I ran into at one of the pilot's social events? Mister handsome green eyes! You should have seen the look on his face when I told him to never tell a redhead SHE can't do something, "You could be cursed forever by the Red Revenge!"

About five years later, I decided to invite some of my balloon pilot friends and their crews to come to my city for an event/competition like the many I had participated in. I began the planning by asking the local aviation community what they thought of my idea to stage an event here. I was laughed at, all the way out the aviation doors. "You can't do that here! You don't know what you're doing. You're a women in a man's field of expertise. You're just a silly air bag pilot. You won't get anyone to come. The City Council and Airport Manager will never allow you to have anything like that here…" Oh my, deep breath. Another bunch of folks that do not realize the power of a redhead when told NO or YOU CAN'T DO THAT. Shameful.

The vicious redhead arguing with the airport manager while air show pilot looks on. Vicious redhead won!

To make this long story short of the adventures in fighting red tape, government employees, elected officials, the good ol' boys aviation network, and the despised airport manager, the name of my event was Balloons Over The Valley Air Festival. It was recognized as a national trend setter in combining hot air balloons with the air show industry. I was invited to speak before the International Council of Airshows annual convention instructing other event organizers how to combine the two.

Early morning launch of hot air balloons.
Balloons Over The Valley Air Festival
Modesto, California.

My event lasted for five years before I threw in the towel. The biggest years saw nearly 70 hot air balloons from all across the U.S., military aircraft from all over the West Coast, military recruiter displays, airshow performers, a ladies parachute team, remote control modeler's aircraft demonstrations, over 100 antique and current aircraft fly-ins for display, helicopter rides, airplane rides, the highest number of daily take-offs and landings recorded in the history of the airport ... it was awesome!

It became a full time job fighting the bureaucratic BS and the good ol' boys year after year. Weather was also a big factor, but money (the lack thereof) was the major factor in deciding not to continue the event. I was tired. And broke. To the dismay of all the pilots and participants, I said I had done enough to prove that redheads should never be told they cannot accomplish what is in their hearts to do.

If you tell a redhead not to do something, she'll do it twice and take pictures.

A quick glance back at history reminds us of cultures that had consistently provoked extreme personalities and unfounded behaviors in redheads by branding them as witches and other assorted labels. As far back as the 4th-5th centuries, tribes of red haired Thracians were feared as bloodthirsty barbarians, extravagant, and impatient as they fought the Ancient Greeks and Romans. Artwork depicts them as <u>Rufus</u>, the common name at that time, for having a red head. That past history has

Fiery & Feisty

instilled generations with a fear of redheads; they must all be witches, fearless, bloodthirsty fighters, or an unusual type of human. Other cultures labeled redheads as sensitive, passionate, headstrong, and rebellious. All of these fears, characteristics, and myths have passed from generation to generation via folklore.

Redheads inexplicably provoke
unexpected, outrageous behavior in everyone.
It's kind of a "Perk."

But wait! Folklore, myths, and hocus pocus have now been pushed aside by modern science. You've already read how science has dispelled several redhead myths. Can science really prove that redheads have fiery, feisty tempers?

By and large, the answer is SORT OF. First the therapists of today would listen attentively to us explain our younger years being constantly taunted and bullied. His/her conclusive observations would note those younger years gave us our emotional thick skin. Redheads learned to deal with anger, frustration, and impatience which evolved into fiery tempers and sharp tongues. Redheads also developed a tolerance of stupidity, and empathy for weak and caring souls. A bit of arrogance developed along with the mastery of overcoming those younger years. All of that might be, but as we leave the therapist's office we know there are still folks out there who are very slow learners and continue to taunt and bully. Fools. The red hair is a warning label to those bullies of any age. Are they too stupid to heed the warning?

How do you handle a redhead's temper?
Gingerly, very gingerly.

What do the scientists say? There are still differing opinions; however, most agree that temper control and emotions are dependent on a wide variety of genetic, environmental, cultural, and personal factors. It is difficult for scientists to measure the storm that will begin to stir in an angry redhead. Further angry storm studies must be undertaken!

Redheads can slam revolving doors.

When the MC1R gene was discovered it opened a huge field of scientific genetic discoveries with just that one particular gene

Fiery & Feisty

alone! New discoveries continue to this day. One of the most fascinating findings was the effect of the MC1R on the body's production of <u>adrenaline</u>.

Adrenaline, also known as epinephrine, is a natural hormone released by the adrenal glands. Stress, fear, or anger will initiate its release into the blood stream to prepare the body for the fight-or-flight response. The heart rate will increase, blood pressure will increase, air passages in the lungs will dilate to allow an increase in oxygen levels, pupils in the eyes will dilate, and blood flow will be redistributed to the larger muscles in the body. All of these responses occur in everyone; however, the MC1R gene in redheads causes a bit different reaction.

Without going into the physiological aspects of the chemicals involved and have you, the reader, nod off from boredom, I will narrow it down to the fact that redheads produce far more adrenaline than non-reds when stress, fear, or anger is experienced; almost double the amount! Once the adrenal glands release this large adrenaline dump into the bloodstream, the redhead experiences the fight-or-flight response much faster than a non-red. This is extremely advantageous in an emergency situation when an event must be evaluated and acted upon immediately. A redheaded nurse or physician in the hospital emergency room or intensive care setting is your best friend when you are in a medical crisis situation. Likewise, a redheaded law enforcement, paramedic, or fire fighter experiences the same response in their occupational situations. Once the situation has been adequately controlled, the adrenaline dissipates quickly and the redhead returns to normal, faster than a non-red.

That fast response from an adrenaline dump also occurs when a redhead is told NO; probably first noticeable in early childhood. There is no clinical/scientific evidence to back this theory; however, ask any parent of a redheaded child and they will surely agree. As that little redhead becomes an adult, the adrenaline response remains. Hopefully, by adulthood the response has been better controlled, but don't be too sure.

Telling an angry redhead to calm down
works as well as trying to baptize a cat.

In 1998, James Wilson, PhD coined the term adrenal fatigue to describe symptoms experienced by individuals in high stress occupations or life situations working over long periods of time. The constant release of adrenaline to handle the stress results in adrenal gland burnout - adrenal fatigue. The medical community and the Endocrine Society stated there is no scientific proof to back this theory and have basically poo-pooed the condition. There is no way to measure adrenal fatigue; therefore it does not exist, it's a myth. Really? Redheads heartily disagree.

Symptoms of adrenal fatigue reported by Wilson in his book (*Adrenal Fatigue: The 21st Century Stress Syndrome*) include:
* tiredness to extreme fatigue
* trouble getting to sleep and waking up
* craving salt and sugar
* unexplained weight loss
* reliance on stimulants such as caffeine
* nonspecific digestive problems

The argument from the medical and scientific community is these symptoms are generic and could be overcome by changes in diet and lifestyle. There is nothing in the literature specifically pointing to redheads succumbing to adrenal fatigue; however, there are plenty of redheads in stressful occupations or situations over many years exhibiting these symptoms. It would make sense to this redheaded author that if we reds use double the amount of adrenaline every time we are stressed or angered, we would certainly be candidates for adrenal burnout at some point.

After all these years post publication of the term, and the increase in the number of patients in high stress occupations complaining of the same symptoms, we can only hope this myth of a medical condition eventually becomes accepted as reality. There is a bit of hope with the younger generation of endocrinologists listening to their (redheaded) patients and agreeing with the possibility of adrenal fatigue. Treatment would then become plausible. The same symptoms are now being recognized as PTSD (Post Traumatic Stress Disorder) in some individuals; however, those individuals also face the same insurance battles for treatment. The medical insurance companies will not cover any testing or specific treatments due to non-recognition of the adrenal fatigue condition, but they are beginning to recognize PTSD, especially in non-military cases.

What do you call a redhead with an attitude?
Normal.

Adrenaline isn't the only mechanism in the fight-or-flight response. <u>Cortisol</u> also plays a primary role as an essential stress hormone. While adrenaline jumps right in by increasing the heart rate, raising the blood pressure, etc. for an immediate response over a short period of time, cortisol also jumps in, but manages things a little differently. Cortisol sends an alarm message to the brain to release stored sugars into the bloodstream for energy needed to fight the stress and puts the immune system on alert. The cortisol alarm also decreases nonessential bodily functions in a fight-or-flight situation: the digestive system, reproductive system, growth systems, etc. Cortisol provides a longer, smoother term of response to the perceived threat.

Both stress hormones return to normal when the stressor has passed. One might label the adrenaline as the "fight" response and the cortisol as the "flight" response.

Redheads don't have BAD tempers,
they have SHARP ones.

If redheads produce more adrenaline than non-reds, do they also produce more cortisol? Both are produced by the adrenal glands, but have different functions as mentioned above. It is surmised that adrenal fatigue relates primarily to the over use and increased levels of adrenaline, not cortisol.

A decrease in cortisol levels is termed adrenal insufficiency. It is a recognized condition/disease because it can be measured and diagnosed with blood tests, unlike adrenal fatigue or PTSD.

Damage or problems with the adrenal glands result in the glands not making enough cortisol which, in turn, leads to a long list of problems. MC1R is also involved with the diagnosis of adrenal insufficiency in redheads. The redhead gene causes defects in how different hormones secreted by the pituitary gland react to other hormones which in turn signal the adrenal glands to produce more cortisol. An interruption of this cascade of events leads to less cortisol production with MC1R as the culprit causing it.

The answer to the initial question then, is no. Redheads do not produce more cortisol, they are more likely to produce LESS and fall victim to adrenal insufficiency. Symptoms of adrenal insufficiency are similar to those experienced by adrenal fatigue; the only difference in diagnosing

Fiery & Feisty

the same symptoms is low cortisol blood levels can be substantiated (measured) by laboratory testing.

MC1R also becomes a discerning factor in the connection between red hair, adrenal insufficiency, hypothyroidism, and Down syndrome, especially in those with Irish or Scottish heritage. It is all about the genetics.

*So, if a redhead goes a bit crazy,
is it called a Ginger Snap?
Asking for a friend.*

Product advertising also plays a part in reinforcing the stereotype that redheads are fiery and have quick tempers. Some redheads are referred to as "matchsticks." Matchsticks start fires. Most matchstick heads have red tips that burst into flame when struck; just like an angry redhead would when challenged. A long standing Australian match company is known as Redheads.

Redheads matchsticks.

Besides redheads being called matchsticks, they might also be called "firecrackers,"

Firecracker.

147

Never Let A Ginger SNAP

especially around the 4th of July. Firecrackers are usually small cylinder shaped tubes packed with an explosive with a bright red cover indicating danger. A short fuse extends from one end of the small cylinder. When the short fuse is lit (perhaps with a red tipped matchstick?), it takes mere seconds for the loud pop of explosion to occur; just like an angry redhead.

*The ire in fire will occur when
a redhead's short fuse is lit.*

Big Red chewing gum advertisements feature multiple lovely red-heads happily chewing the cinnamon flavored gum.

At this point, is it safe to say that redheads are fiery and feisty? YES! Based on the studies and evidence the blame can again be squarely placed on that MC1R rascal. As a reminder, the red hair is a warning! If you challenge, confront or threaten a redhead, remember, they have an itchy trigger finger on their adrenaline gun with its cortisol backup. Always proceed with caution.

*It takes a special kind of stupid
to piss off a redhead and expect calm.*

Chapter 12
Fire & Ice

Fire and ice - like Hell fire and Holy water

I have published eleven non-fiction books over the past ten years and I am fortunate enough to have a small gathering of book groupies who have read all of them. When I told them I was deviating from World War II history to a lighter subject, one of my groupies told me, "SEX SELLS - throw some sex in it!" Of course, the sex research began immediately!

What do you think of or visualize when you hear the word RED? What do you feel when you see something that is red? Fire engines are (usually) red; you might think of fire, danger, and fear. Your heart rate may increase with the fight-or-flight release of adrenaline. STOP signs and lights are red to grab your attention, slow you down, although many fail to heed them. Reactions are quicker and more forceful at the sight of red, often motivating us to take immediate action.

A big red heart shaped Valentine's box with your favorite chocolates will surely release an emotional response of warmth, comfort, and love. Blood vessels will dilate to give those "warm fuzzy" feelings which often lead to passion and intimacy (sex!). Red is the color of cupid as well as the devil: love and hate.

The color red in nature is most often beautiful, intense, vibrant, loud, exudes strength, and power. It can also be a symbol of danger. A red sky at sunrise or sunset can be spectacularly beautiful or frightfully menacing. Remember the old sailors' adage of "Red sky in the morn', sailors forlorn, stormy weather ahead." Or, "Red sky at night, sailors' delight, good weather ahead."

Red is the color of energy and action. It is the color most often used in advertising because it is bold, eye catching, and draws you in. It is always easier to remember the product(s) with a red label: Campbell's Soup, Red Bull, Lego, Staples, Colgate, Tesla, Target, Dr. Pepper, Coca Cola, Pepsi, Sara Lee, Ray Ban, Canon, Firestone, Coleman, Lay's… the list is long. Take your own survey of red labels next time you walk the grocery store isles. Which ones catch your eye?

So what does all this have to do with redheads and sex? Reread the last couple of paragraphs and pick out all the adjectives describing the color red. Fire, danger, fear, emotional, warmth, comfort, love, passion, hate, beautiful, intense, vibrant, loud, strength, power, spectacular, frightful, menacing, energy, action, anger, bold, eye catching. Wouldn't you agree, these are all terms describing redheads with some also describing sex?!

It's a redhead thing.
If you've dated a redhead, raise your glass.
If not, raise your standards.

There are stories in trashy and not so trashy publications of questionable studies with the topic of redheads and their apparent wild sexual activities. Of course, there is little mention of redheaded men in these publicized studies. Instead, it always seems to be about the redheaded women, more than any other hair color, those slutty, lusty redheads who are wild in bed and orgasm several times a week. Oh, good grief! Consider the source for these bogus claims and unscientific studies. Here are a couple of examples:

In August 2006, the British tabloid newspaper *Daily Mail* published an article about a German study undertaken by a Hamburg sex researcher, Professor Dr. Werner Habermehl. The Professor purportedly interviewed "hundreds" of German women, after first separating them by hair color, then questioned each of them about their sex lives.

Never Let A Ginger SNAP

He reported the following results: "The sex lives of women with red hair were clearly more active than those with other hair color, with more partners and having sex more often than the average. The research shows that the fiery redhead certainly lives up to her reputation. Women who dyed their hair red from another color are signaling they were looking for a partner. Even women in a fixed relationship are letting their partners know they are unhappy if they dye their hair red. They are saying that they are looking for something better." Habermehl added, "Blondes may have more fun, but redheads have more sex."

Gentlemen may prefer blondes or brunettes,
but it takes a real man to handle a redhead.

Several "red flags" pop up with this study and its authenticity. First of all, who is this sex research professor anyway and exactly where is he located? Where was this study conducted; a university, his living room or his bedroom? This author found very little, if any, information about Dr. Werner Habermehl other than his article published in the tabloid newspaper as opposed to a medical or scientific journal. Secondly, where are the statistics? How many actually participated? How

Fire & Ice

many women in each color group? Were all the women true redheads or were some bottle reds included? How did he establish the statements about those who dyed their hair red? Where are the percentages and comparisons? Hmmmm. Kinda stinks. Bogus.

Redheads don't play well with stupid people.

Another questionable study done in 2013 by the dating site Match.com boasted some pretty outrageous claims about female redheads and their sexual activities. There were 5,300 unmarried men and women who responded to the survey; however, there were only 186 women that actually completed the questionnaire who may or may not have been true redheads. One of the questions on the study was, "Currently, what color is your hair?" This question alone likely falsified the study outcome by mixing the natural redheads with sexually adventurous women who might have picked the red color because they thought it made them look more fiery. The dubious results published "...redheaded women orgasm more than any other hair color... 41 percent of redheads allegedly had orgasms 90 to 100 percent of the time versus 36 percent of blondes, 34 percent of brunettes and 29 percent of women with black hair...thought more about sex...had more threesomes, one-night stands and friends-with-benefits situations than people with other hair colors."

Dr. Helen Fisher, an advisor on the study, was quoted regarding the results, "Red hair is novel, and men and women are turned on by people who are novel and different." Those results were published on other dating services and websites, magazines, and tabloid rags, with the headline, **"Redheads Have More Fun!"** There was an obvious increase in responses to the dating sites as well as publication sales which was obviously the apparent purpose for the "study" in the first place. Bogus.

Along comes psychologist and author Christine Baumanns with her followup insight about redheads and sex. She theorizes men are attracted to the color red, especially on a woman; red lipstick, a slinky red dress, and of course, red hair. The attraction to female redheads may be due to their rarity. Baumanns states, "Red stands for passion and when a man sees a redhead he will think he is dealing with a woman who won't mess around, and gets straight to the point when it comes to sex." I wonder if Baumanns is a redhead? What facts or studies did she base her statements on? Hopefully, it wasn't the previous bogus studies.

Following up on Baumanns' claim that men are attracted to redheads, the term rutiluphilia comes to mind; the name for a fetish or attraction to redheads. Such a person would be a rutiluphile. If you can figure out how to pronounce these terms, feel free to use them next time it would be appropriate to do so, or when you become enamored at the sight of a drop dead gorgeous redhead!

Good girls go to heaven.
Redheads go wherever they damn well please.

It would stand to reason, in this author's humble opinion, that with all the societal awareness, whether true or false, that redheads are overly sexual and perhaps even promiscuous, it might give us reds the go ahead to live up to those expectations!? Right? This redheaded author will not detail, affirm, nor deny any personal experiences past or present, in collaboration with that statement! No pictures either! Sorry.

*You'd find it much easier
to be bad than good
if you had red hair.*

So, are there any legitimate, scientific studies about these redhead/sex claims? Not much published that this author could find. However, there are several claims from science based studies regarding the MC1R gene (again) that would be helpful in drawing sexy conclusions.

The previous discussion about how redheads release adrenaline in fight-or-flight situations might also be a positive clue to heightened awareness and sensitivity in passionate (sexual) situations. The response to physical stimuli is faster and stronger than in those without the MC1R gene.

Recall the studies by Dr. Daniel Sessler at the Cleveland Clinic mentioned earlier. His work concluded redheads feel more pain (dental) but are more resistant to other types of pain (topical stings). Because of the MC1R gene, redheads process pain responses differently; so, it follows that redheads would also respond differently to pleasure. The MC1R gene has an effect on the brain's release of endorphins which provide the feeling of pain relief as well as the feelings of pleasure. These facts would certainly fit the claim that redheads enjoy sex more, or have more orgasms. Is it that mutated rascal MC1R tickling those endorphins? Whoopee!

It's not the hair that turns men on,
it's the spirit that redheads exude through their pores.

Pheromones play a significant part in our daily lives. Pheromones are actually chemicals that think they are external sex hormones. Internal hormones released by the body have a direct effect on the individual secreting them. In all of nature, external hormones have a direct effect on the opposite sex by triggering sexual arousal for the purpose of mating (sex). When the pheromones are secreted via the sebaceous glands, the opposite sex responds with a bit of an adrenaline rush, an endorphin release, an increase in heart rate, and a feeling of euphoria. These chemicals are primarily present in axillary sweat. There is no specific or discernible scent of the pheromones noticed from most humans. Those of the opposite sex have an olfactory sense that detects the pheromone scent, sends a message to the brain that action is imminent and foreplay might begin (sex).

Now, here is what is a bit different for redheads and their pheromones. As early as 1886, French author Dr. Augustin Galopin recorded his theory of women and the specific natural scents they give off. In his book, *Le Parfum de la Femme,* he proclaimed women with red or chestnut colored hair gave off a particular scent unlike women with other colors of hair. The particular scent Dr. Galopin noted was <u>ambergris,</u> an earthy, sensual scent. Although his conclusions were based solely on experimentation, observation, and his acute sense of smell versus any type of scientific testing, many years later, they were proved to be correct.

Le Parfum de la Femme
Dr. Augustin Galopin,
author, 1886.

(Author's interesting side note: Ambergris is sperm whale vomit or poop (conflicting scientific theories as to which end it is expelled from). While wet, it smells like nasty sewer poop. As it dries, the ambergris has a more pleasant "musky" scent. <u>Ambrein</u> is an odorless alcohol extracted from the dried ambergris and used in perfumes to make the

scent last longer. The finest, most expensive perfumes only use white ambergris, often referred to as "sea gold." Early civilizations used it as incense, an aphrodisiac, and in medicines. Synthetic chemicals are now used as an imitation ambrein; however, the more exclusive perfumeries still process ambergris for the ambrein. White ambergris usually sells for $30/Gm. depending on

Chunks of ambergris - whale poop or vomit?

quality. A recent 130 lb. chunk of white ambergris, found by a fisherman, is valued at $3 million. That poor whale must have been severely constipated to let loose with a 130 lb. poop ball. So next time you dab on that $500 per 2 ounce bottle of perfume, keep in mind it was made with whale poop!)

A trucker will slow down for a blonde,
stop for a brunette,
but he'll back up 500 yards for a redhead.

In his 1996 book, *The Redheaded Encyclopedia,* author Stephen Douglas basically concurs with Dr. Galopin's 1886 findings and combines them with updated science. He reiterates redheads have a scent of their own created by their release of pheromones. The scent can also change with the redhead's emotions. Douglas called redhead's scent a sweet, musky essence released by the skin, not just the axillary sweat. There is more skin surface than armpit surface so there would likely be a considerably larger amount of pheromones released on any unsuspecting member of the opposite sex. Poor guy, under the spell of the mysterious sexy redhead, doesn't stand a chance. The fire was lit with the first whiff! Wouldn't this make a great trashy romance novel? Whale poop and the lusty redhead?

Redheads are said to be children of the moon,
thwarted by the sun, addicted to sex and sugar.

With all this sexy talk comes the locker room vulgarities. In grade school the taunts were: "I'd

Fire & Ice

rather be dead than have red on the head." In the adult world, the taunt is: "RED on the head equals FIRE in bed." Reds endure many nicknames about the color of their head hair so it should be no surprise that they must also endure the humiliating, offensive, trash talk about their pubic hair. Evidently, it does not occur to the locker room mentality that most all men and women have the same color hair upper, lower and all around: head and pubic area as well as arms, armpits, back, and legs. The exception to this natural phenomena would be if the head hair color comes from a bottle. Only the truly vain dye the eyebrows and pubic hair to match the head hair. Really? Yes, they do.

Red hair comes from sugar and lust.

The most common question coming from the locker room boys (young and older) or the elbow benders at the local bar: "Does the carpet match the drapes?" Translation: "Is your pubic hair the same color as the hair on your head?" How about, "Are you Irish all the way down?" Or, as they point to your lower region, "Ya got hot sauce down there?" Along the same lines, "I like carrot muffins for breakfast." A snappy female redheaded comeback, while pointing at the offensive offender's crotch might be, "Ya, well I like big ginger balls at Christmas time - too bad for you."

It's not a party until the redheads show up.

Perhaps the most tawdry reference to the nether regions is the term "fire crotch." The term was featured several years ago in multiple tabloid rags when a Hollywood celebrity couple (she was a redhead, he was not) aired their dirty sexual laundry in public after a breakup. Evidently, fans of the misguided redheaded celebrity picked up on the term and thought it useful when questioning redheaded date prospects. I'm fairly certain injuries would have been incurred when that approach was utilized. Never underestimate the power of a redhead's verbal comebacks in any type of situation.

Redheads are the reason Santa has a naughty list!

We will move forward from the fire crotch redheads to the ice queen redheads. If you have been paying close attention to the educational

Fire & Ice

material presented so far, you should expect that ol' MC1R gene to have some say in the way redheads respond to temperature changes. And it most certainly does! Remember Dr. Daniel Sessler and his research findings regarding redheads, MC1R, and pain? While researching pain tolerance came the revelation of thermal temperature differences in redheads, briefly mentioned earlier. He and his team studied 60 redheads and 60 brunettes to determine their reactions to temperature changes. Testing using external heat and cold pressures in relation to pain tolerance found redheads began to feel pain at a temperature of 43°F. Brunettes tolerated temperatures as low as freezing, 32°F, before feeling pain. The conclusion was, redheads feel hot and cold temperature changes faster and with greater intensity than non-redheads.

Further investigation and studies of the MC1R gene found the temperature detector part of the gene may become over-activated in redheads which makes them more sensitive to environmental thermal extremes. A redhead can detect cold weather changes faster than a meteorologist! You've heard the stories of grandma predicting an approaching cold storm because her knees were "acting up"? Grandma was probably a redhead before her red locks turned snowy white.

In the blockbuster movie *Frozen*, the two animated sisters are Anna and Elsa. Anna has red hair while sister Elsa, the Snow Queen, has white hair. All that ice and snow surely made Elsa's red hair turn white as her redheaded body adjusted to the icy cold conditions. Did the animators know about redheads versus cold? Just a point to ponder! Oh just, "Let It Go!"

Elsa the Snow Queen (L) & Anna (R) the redhead.

Redheads always seem to be cold. Sweaters, jackets, and blankets are nearby no matter what the season or outside air temperature. Perhaps this might explain it: Redheaded women have lower core blood temperatures than non-redheaded women; three degrees lower in fact. The recognized normal, by medical studies, is 98.6°F.

Fire & Ice

Redheaded women are normally 95.3-97.5°F. A temperature of 98.6° for a redhead should be considered a low-grade fever; a 100° temperature is serious cause for alarm. It is nearly impossible to get the doctors and nurses to understand this fact. There is hope; look how long it took the dental community to realize redheads need 20% more topical anesthetic.

Redheads may be cold all the time; however, they also do not tolerate high heat. Perhaps this is the body's way of warning the redhead to stay out of the sun especially in the hottest part of the day? An inside and outside air temperature of 75° would be ideal for the redheads year 'round!

Redheads are like the American flag -
Red, White, & Blue.

Chapter 13
Redhead Potpourri

*Blondes may be noticed but
redheads are never forgotten.*

Redhead's Yellow Teeth

Many years ago I contracted hepatitis from contaminated hamburger meat at a nearby fast food establishment. Hepatitis is a very unpleasant malady and takes forever to recover. I was not responding well to treatment (typical redhead) and was getting sicker everyday. I was transferred to the University hospital where more elaborate tests and procedures were done, then slipped into a hepatic coma. Things were pretty dire and my family was notified of my impending doom. After a week in the coma, I rallied and remained hospitalized for several more weeks. It was an unpleasant experience to say the least.

When the liver is sick, bile is excreted into the skin giving off a bright yellow-orange glow to all skin surfaces and the whites of the eyes. With my rusty red hair, yellow eyeballs, and skin, I looked like a circus freak.

One afternoon shortly after I had rallied from the coma, my mother traveled the distance to the University hospital for a short visit. All visitors had to put on a cover gown and gloves before entering my isolation room. She had not seen me since before I had been first diagnosed then transferred. She was totally shocked by my appearance and verbally stumbled a bit to find the proper words. "Wow, your teeth have never looked so white," she happily exclaimed. She was right, my teeth always seemed to look yellow tinged no matter what I did to have pearly whites.

Redheads have such pale skin or pale pink tones, there is very little contrast between the light skin and the color of teeth. The darker the skin, the whiter the appearance of the teeth. With the yellow-orange hepatitis coloring, my teeth actually did look white; first time ever, never again.

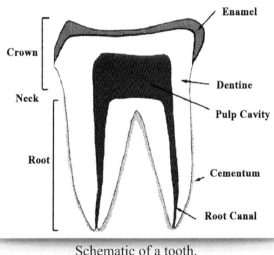

Schematic of a tooth.
Note the dentin area.

The scientific explanation blames redheads yellow hued teeth on the unique anatomy of their tooth surface. First of all, the tooth enamel itself is thinner than on any other hair colored person. Secondly, the dentin, the calcified layer of the tooth under the enamel, is yellowish or grayish in natural color. The yellow color shows through the thin enamel layer giving the constant appearance of yellowed teeth.

No amount of bleaching, or whitening agents can change this and may harm the tooth surface in attempting to do so. As we redheads age, the discoloration will likely increase due to stains from coffee, tea, cola, wine. The stains may be lightened, but the original yellow dentin will remain showing through.

With an unlimited budget for non-essential cosmetic purposes, redheads may resort to veneers for a pearly white mouthful of glorious white teeth. Otherwise, wear a darker colored lipstick along with a bronze blush to create contrast between skin and teeth. Sorry, I have no recommendations for what the male reds should do; lipstick wouldn't go over very well, neither would the bronze blush.

Blondes may be wild & brunettes might be true,
but you never know just what a redhead will do.

Redhead's Sense of Scents

I love the fragrance of garden roses. My garden has over fifty different types and colors so I enjoy a variety of different rosy fragrances. My two favorites are a pale pink with a soft, sweet fragrance and a violet purple with a strong, tangy, fresh fragrance. No perfume counter has ever come close to the classic rose fragrance I like, but they have tried.

On a shopping excursion long ago, I was delighted to find a body lotion and cologne that advertised the scent of fresh cut roses. A sniff of the contents confirmed it was the delightful scent of a soft pink rose. I purchased a bottle of the lotion and a spritz bottle of the cologne. Later, after a luxurious shower, I slathered the new body lotion all over and enjoyed smelling like a lovely pink rose… for about 15 minutes, then I caught the odor of dead dandelions. Honestly, nothing ever smells quite right on me. Is it another curse on the redhead? How? Why?

We all have a microscopic layer of film covering our skin surfaces. The term for this layer is the skin mantle. Even though microscopic, this mantle is like a shield or barrier to bacteria, viruses, and other harmful contaminates to the skin. It also keeps the skin hydrated and moisturized. The mantle is made up of sebum, the waxy, oily substance secreted by the sebaceous glands located within the layers of our skin. Those sebaceous glands are also responsible for secreting pheromones, and sweat which all contribute to the formation of the mantle and give it an acidic pH level.

If the acidic mantle is damaged from poor skin care, harsh cleansers, an injury, or sunburn, it takes up to two weeks to repair itself. In the meantime, the skin can become dehydrated (from the sunburn or overall dehydration), oily with acne, or sensitive to the touch.

In redheads, male and female, the mantle is much more acidic than non-reds. Application of scented lotions, perfumes, colognes, or scented oils react with the highly acidic mantle and the fragrance is changed or dissipated altogether. Think of this as a chemical reaction happening on your skin; the acidic mantle is fighting with the chemicals in the fragrances for the win! Too bad the win is the scent change of the lovely, expensive perfume or lotion you just applied, to the smell of dead dandelions. Splash on more and the same thing will happen over and over. Some reds spray cologne or perfume on their hair instead of the neck or wrists to avoid the scent change on the skin. Depending on what chemicals or oils are in the fragrance, damage to the hair follicles can occur. Be careful.

As mentioned earlier, a redhead's temper and emotions can also change their natural scent. When a perfume or scented lotion is applied and mixes with the acidic mantle during those particular times, there will surely be a change in the fragrance (dead dandelions again?).

Not only do redheads smell different, many possess a greater sense of smell than non-reds. Some redheads view this ability as another curse while others feel it is a blessing in the jobs they do. Hundreds of redheads confirm they have this unusual sense of smell. Although this author did not find any specific scientific proof of this, it would stand to reason as factual, based on how many other odd things seem normal for reds!

Hundreds of studies have been undertaken in recent years to better understand the human sense of smell. It is the only sense that affects the memory and emotion part of the brain. The unpleasant scent of something alerts the brain of danger - the smell of smoke, rotten food, infection, chemicals - so the body can avoid any potential exposure or damage.

Pleasant, as well as unpleasant, scents can evoke past memories from childhood, lost loves, nature... As mentioned in the previous chapter, the brain can decipher the scent of pheromones between two people attracted to each other. Perfume companies design fragrances with sex in mind. Their advertising messages are most often sexual in nature.

The most pleasant scents discovered by testing are utilized to enhance the thousands of products we humans use everyday. If it smells good, it must be good, so we purchase the products: soaps, detergents, fabric softeners, dish soap, air fresheners, pet food, kitty litter, shampoo, deodorants, bath products, lotions... the list is endless.

The sense of smell and taste are closely linked. Researchers found 80% of the flavors we taste come from what we smell. The taste buds on our tongues can only identify sweet, sour, bitter, and salty; the remaining "tastes" are actually distinguished by smell.

The loss of the ability to smell can be temporary, such as a stuffy nose from a cold or allergies, or an indicator of a potentially serious condition. It was discussed earlier that redheads and their MC1R gene have a higher possibility for developing Parkinson's disease. The diminishing sense of smell for no particular reason can also be an early indicator of Parkinson's disease years before motor skill abnormalities become evident. Alzheimer's disease also fits this category.

That darn MC1R gene strikes again.

Redheads vs Insects

I flew the hot air balloon for twelve years. Balloons do not launch from or land at airports (only on rare occasions). Instead, we launch from pastures, soccer fields, school yards, large parking lots... Where ever the wind takes us, we look for landing sites in any open field or area free of overhead power lines, obstructions, or farm animals. What did all these launch and landing sites have in common? FLYING BITING BUGS!

Mosquitoes were the worst. I swear they swarmed me, attacked any exposed skin surface, then left me a lumpy, bumpy, itchy mess. I can still hear those little buzzing buggers around my head.

Never Let A Ginger SNAP

Preparing to land in an open alfalfa field. Scared up a flock of birds. Mosquitoes lurking to attack.

My non-redheaded passengers never seemed to be bothered by them while I was constantly under attack. Was it my red hair? Are redheads mosquito magnets? There is a rumor out there that redheads are bitten by flying insects more than others. Fact or fiction? Let's investigate.

Mosquitoes are not attracted to color, they are attracted to smell. It is the female mosquito that bites, not the male. (Are female mosquitoes angry redheads?) She needs human blood to develop fertile eggs and is always on the hunt for the perfect smell. There are more than 175 known species of mosquitos in the United States alone, some fairly dangerous, in that they can spread the deadly West Nile virus.

Researchers have been hard at work trying to determine what particular compounds and odors people release that attract or repel the biting buzzing buggers. Scientists have determined that genetics (85%) play an important role in who is most susceptible to the bites. Are you thinking it's that MC1R gene again? Draw your own conclusions.

Mosquitoes have a tremendous sense of smell. If you are releasing the right scents, they can zero in on you from as far away as over 160 feet. Their favorite smell from a human is carbon dioxide (CO_2) which is expelled when we exhale. Large people (adult size) exhale larger amounts of CO_2 compared to smaller people or children. If that large person is exercising strenuously, the mosquitoes are attracted to the CO_2, the movement, and the scent of lactic acid being given off through the skin's sweat glands. If you are lucky enough to metabolize cholesterol quickly, the byproducts are released through the skin and what mosquito wouldn't like a dash of cholesterol in her bloody meal? Like steak with a dash of ketchup!

There are several other types of compounds released via exhalation or skin excretion which attract the little buzzards, but CO_2 and lactic acid are their favorites. So how can we repel them?

The most effective way to repel them is to cover the scents your body is transmitting. You can't very well cover the invisible CO2 you exhale, but you can cover the scents your skin is releasing. Many repellents are available on the market today to do just that: cover the scents. Products containing DEET (diethyltoluamide) are the most effective today. These products have an oil base and a light scent unattractive to mosquitoes. Sprayed on skin surfaces, the oil base adheres to the skin to mask the scents of lactic acid, uric acid, cholesterol, acetone, etc. and lasts about five hours. The scent of the DEET product may also be enough to disguise the scent of CO2 being exhaled. Be sure to wash this off with soap and water when you go inside to avoid any potential skin reaction to the chemical (you know how redheads skin reacts to EVERYTHING).

A newer repellent in the United States is marketed as Cutter Advanced which contains picaridin. It is just as effective as DEET, odorless with a less oily feel. Another newer product, metofluthrin, is not applied to the skin. It can be used as a paper strip in a patio area or in a small container clipped to a belt or on the clothing. It has a battery powered fan to release the repellent into the surrounding area. It is marketed and sold as DeckMate Mosquito Repellent.

Redhead Potpourri

Avon's Skin-So-Soft has also been marketed as a mosquito repellent in the United States. It contains the chemical IR3535 and has been found by research to be much less effective than DEET and the newer products mentioned.

Don't want all those chemicals on your skin? Try citronella, peppermint, geranium, or cedar scents in candles or oils. Oil of eucalyptus lasts longer and boasts protection similar to low concentrations of DEET.

One of my hot air balloon passengers, a science teacher at the nearby college, suggested I try taking B complex vitamins the night before an early morning flight. The thiamine (B1) is excreted through the skin and mosquitoes do not like the smell. It worked! Maybe not 100%, but it made a remarkable difference with less bites.

Now, if you think about the previous chapters in which it was spelled out how redheads process things differently than others and have more of an acidic skin mantle, stronger secretions of pheromones, stronger chemical reactions occurring to change the scent of fragrances, etc. etc. etc., do you agree or disagree that mosquitoes like redheads more?

Never Let A Ginger SNAP

*Some time ago, a cobra bit a redhead.
After five days of excruciating pain, the cobra died.*

Now, what about bees, hornets, yellow jackets; all stinging bee types? Are they attracted to the red hair, think we're flowers and sting us more than others? Are we bee magnets? Supposedly, that is a myth; however, ask any redhead how many times he/she has been stung by a bee and you may doubt the myth theory.

Honey bees are not attracted to the smell of humans as such, but to their sweet scents of perfume, hair products, lotions, and deodorants. Bees depend more on their sight than on smell to locate pollen and nectar then return it to the hive. When bees are flying, they see better. They can see three dimensionally and judge depth. Honey bees have a much broader range of color vision due to the anatomy of their eyes; two different types of eyes each with separate functions. The eyes help the bee maintain stability and navigate while flying as well as enable it to judge light intensity and see ultra-violet light in the flower colors.

Honey bee. Usually shades of brown in color.

Redhead Potpourri

The ability to see ultraviolet light is called <u>bee vision</u>. Many patterns on flowers are invisible to the human eye due to our inability to see ultraviolet light. Humans base their color combinations on red, blue, and green while bees base their colors on ultraviolet light, blue and green - that's why bees cannot differentiate the color red.

If a honey bee is circling a redhead, it isn't attracted to the red hair. It might be the floral shampoo or hair product or flowery perfume it detects. If the bee stings the redhead, it is likely in a defensive mode protecting a nearby hive or food source or simply feels threatened. If you are wearing a dark color, the bee will naturally go into a defensive mode as you represent a predator and you will be stung. Why do you think beekeepers always wear white covers and head gear? White is usually not a threat to the bees.

Worker honey bees are females (well, that just figures!). They gather the pollen and nectar to feed the colony back at the hive producing the

Bee keeper ready to tend her bees.

honey. These worker honey bees can only sting once. The stinger is barbed and cannot be pulled back by the honey bee. As the bee pulls away, part of its digestive tract attached to the stinger is pulled off, causing a rupture of the abdomen which kills the bee instantly. The stinger continues to imbed itself deeper into the skin pumping the acidic toxin <u>melittin</u> into the victim for several minutes. An alarm pheromone is also emitted by the dying bee. This alerts other nearby worker bees of the perceived danger to the hive which, in turn, causes them to mount a defensive stance.

If stung by a honey bee, it is essential to remove the stinger as quickly as possible to stop the continued injection of the toxin and other substances which cause the pain, itching, and swelling. If a hive is nearby, move away as quickly as you can as the bees are in attack mode and you will be stung multiple times. They are in a suicide defensive mode (little kamikazes) to protect their hive and queen.

Without the honey bee, we humans could not survive, our ecosystem would collapse. At least ninety huge commercial crops depend on bee pollination for survival: almonds, apples, berries, cherries, avocados, citrus, squash, vegetables, and

Redhead Potpourri

many more. Be nice to the honey bees! Do not use pesticides! Do not kill them!

If the bees buzzing around you are big bumblebees, hornets, wasps, or yellow jackets, be aware they are much more aggressive than honey bees. Their alkaline stings are much more painful and can make you ill. They retain their stinger and do not die like the honey bees. These bees get defensive protecting their nests which have no honey, but eggs with future offspring. They are useless and serve no essential purpose. Leave them alone and they will leave you alone. Throwing rocks at a big hornets nest is never a good idea. Take my word for it. Honestly - TAKE MY WORD FOR IT!

Hornet, Yellow Jacket, or Wasp. Usually black with yellow stripes.

Huge hornets nest.
DO NOT
THROW ROCKS
AT IT!
(or anything else!)

Never Let A Ginger SNAP

If you have been stung one time or multiple times by any type of bee, a hypersensitivity may develop which could lead to a more severe reaction to any further stings such as <u>anaphylactic shock</u> - a live threatening reaction requiring emergent treatment. Carry an EpiPen (epinephrine), shown below, for just such an emergency and know how to use it.

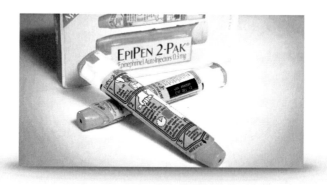

Just like bees, if you tease a redhead
a storm inside her will start to stir.
When the storm rages, it will show no mercy
to man nor beast.
And an EpiPen will not help you!

Chapter 14

Redhead Oddities

Being a redhead and having blonde moments
is just our way of multi-tasking -
don't be jealous!

Skin problems and sensitivities have been discussed in earlier chapters but here are a few other strange things redheads experience:

Metal Sensitivity

Costume jewelry looks lovely on anyone else, but besides the fake stones, the metal used is often nickel. Wearing rings, earrings, bracelets, necklaces, belt buckles, eyeglass frames, or cheap body piercings may commonly cause a red, itchy rash on redheads at the point of contact with the metal. Recall that redhead's skin mantle is naturally more acidic than non-reds. The protective acidic mantle detects the nickel as a harmful substance, sends a message to the immune system which jumps into action to protect and defend, concluding the battle with the itchy red rash. That reaction usually begins within hours or up to several days during or after exposure. Any future contact with a nickel based item will likely cause

Never Let A Ginger SNAP

more of an immediate allergic reaction, i.e. the red itchy rash may become a swollen, hivey mess in need of medical care. Allergic reactions to nickel are also common in non-reds and thought by some medical/scientist folks to be inherited.

Copper and brass are also common metals used in jewelry, especially the cheap stuff. It is also used as a filler with gold. Copper is notorious for reacting to the redhead's high acidic skin mantle. It causes oxidation resulting in the blackening of the copper and discoloration to the skin; usually an ugly green tint. Copper is used in many other items besides jewelry because it does not rust, but it will turn green from the oxidation process. Brass will also oxidize and discolors in similarity to copper.

Redheads (and non-reds) can save themselves from these metal allergy discomforts by paying closer attention to the contents of the metal in the jewelry items they are purchasing. If the rings, earrings, or body piercings are not high quality metals or have nickel, copper, or brass filler, there will be problems. The best metals for sensitive skin are platinum (95% platinum & 5% iridium), titanium, gold (24K is 99.5% pure gold, 18K and 14K have another alloy mixed in, usually copper or brass for color). Hypoallergenic metal is usually

Redheaded Oddities

sterling silver or surgical stainless steel. Sterling silver stamped .925 indicates it is 92.5% silver and does not contain any nickel. It is also resistant to corrosion; it does not tarnish like silver alone will do.

After experiencing my earlobes swelling three times normal size from earrings containing nickel, I am more vigilant in what the pierced posts are made of. I also ask the jeweler to apply a sealant on the posts to be totally sure they do not cause any allergic reactions. Of course, if you aren't purchasing quality jewelry, there are simple ways to protect your poor ears from problems. Apply two or three coats of clear nail polish to the earring posts and allow to thoroughly dry. Reapply when needed. Or, dip the posts in Vaseline if you will only be wearing the earrings for a short time. This is a bit messy and doesn't last very long, but it does work and saves your ears from a nasty reaction.

Static Shocks

It seems that everything I touch gives me a shock and other redheads complain of the same thing. Standing near a radio causes static over the musical program until I move away. I do not, however, glow in the dark with sparks shooting off my red head, or at least no one has ever mentioned it to me. Several resource sites refer to "some people seem to carry a higher static charge than others." Those "some people" are likely redheads.

Could this be a redhead carrying a static charge?!

Static occurs when electric charges accumulate on an object's surface after two materials rub against each other. Walking across a thick carpet with leather shoes will cause invisible electrons from the carpet to jump all over you. The more friction you cause by walking across that carpet, the more electrons you acquire as well as giving you an increased negative charge. Your hair and skin accumulate the electric charges until they can be discharged. Your body surface can easily be charged with 20,000 to 25,000 volts and you don't feel a thing! YIKES! You're sorta like a walking

Redheaded Oddities

invisible lightening bolt or a stun gun. A stun gun might have 50,000 volts or more. To discharge this voltage, when you touch something metal or anything that is positively charged, ZZZZAAAAPPPP you get shocked. The shock is the result of the electrons rapidly moving off you to the metal.

If the air is dry and cold, the electrons are jumpier and buildup quicker on the skin surface. Warmer weather and moisture in the air or moisture on your skin (from moisturizing lotion or sweat) cause the electrons to slide off you quickly and reduce the static charge; you will still receive a shock when you touch metal, it just won't be as painful.

To help minimize or prevent these shocks, reduce the friction between objects by wearing rubber soled shoes or go barefoot, minimize the amount of nylon and polyester you're wearing in clothing, and in dry, wintry conditions apply moisturizers to the skin frequently and conditioner to the hair. Humidifiers in the home are also helpful when the air is dry.

Well, that's all well and good information for normal people, but doesn't really explain why redheads seem to have more, larger, painful shocks as well as causing static on radios. The explanation: It's our HAIR!!

All hair is composed of keratin, as mentioned earlier in the Hairy chapter. Keratin in red hair has twice as much sulphur as in blonde or brunette hair. Hair also contains the minerals and metals of calcium, magnesium, iron, copper, and zinc. All metals conduct electricity. Copper, magnesium, iron, and zinc are all excellent conductors of electricity. Red hair strands are thicker than other colors, thus contain more of these minerals and metals.

As a redhead collects static electrons, the hair (full of more minerals and metals than others) as well as the acidic skin, those 20,000 to 25,000 volts may be a relatively low number. So obviously, when we touch something metal, the shock will be greater than what others experience.

Are we lightening rods? Are we attracting all that electricity? Wellll, it isn't that we attract the electricity, it is that our skin and hair seem to be able to hold more of a charge than others. Lightening rods do not attract lightening, they actually redirect the electric current into the ground when struck by a bolt. So by that definition maybe we are similar to lightening rods! We can

hold the charge on our skin and in our hair, then discharge it on something with a positive charge - painfully. But don't forget, we also process pain differently than others!

Endometriosis

This section may or may not be of interest to the male readers or even the male reds. But, it might be worth the read in order to help understand the female reds' monthly behavior if they are afflicted with this condition.

Endometriosis is a chronic, painful disorder with uterine tissue developing in areas of the female body other than the uterus (the baby carriage). Many people confuse the two terms endometrium and endometriosis. Endometrium is the lining inside the uterine wall. Every month the lining thickens in preparation for receiving a fertilized egg. If none is received, the lining sheds and menses (the period or monthly curse) occurs.

Endometriosis has the same type of tissue found in the uterus. Pieces of the tissue clump together and make themselves at home outside the uterus, usually somewhere in the pelvic area - ovaries, fallopian tubes, bowel, bladder. These clumps of tissue are termed endometrial implants. They respond to the monthly hormonal shifts as if they were in the uterus by bleeding into the surrounding tissue which will later lead to a buildup of scar tissue. This bleeding, in turn, causes cramping, pelvic pain, painful intercourse, irregular periods, or excessive monthly menstrual bleeding. It can also cause infertility in 30-50% of women, as well as an association with other health conditions such as asthma, allergies, multiple sclerosis, hypothyroidism, chronic fatigue syndrome, fibromyalgia, or ovarian and breast cancer. As mentioned in a previous chapter, there is a definite link between redheads and Parkinson's disease, melanoma, and endometriosis.

Redheaded Oddities

Ancient Ayurvedic medicine practitioners linked women with red hair to having painful disorders of the womb. One in ten women in the world have endometriosis. Some of those women experience little or no discomfort while others want to crawl in a deep, dark hole with sanitary supplies, pain killers, and a heating pad for a week. Those would likely be the redheads.

There is no known cause of endometriosis, but it is highly likely certain genes (MC1R again?) predispose women to the condition. Risk factors have been identified as those features you are born with and include the following:

* No prior pregnancies, early onset menses, late menopause.
* Being taller and/or thinner than most women.
* Family history of endometriosis raises risk nearly six-fold (mother, sister, daughter).
* Caucasian or Asian.
** Having red hair, freckles, sun sensitivity, or pre-cancerous skin moles.

Perhaps the largest study undertaken to determine a correlation between natural hair color and the incidence of endometriosis has been the Nurses Health Study II with a ten year follow-up. This study also acknowledged other cross-sectional studies of women with natural red hair claiming coagulation (clotting) alterations and immune functions possibly linked with the diagnosis of endometriosis.

Initially 90,065 women (nurses) between the ages of 25 to 42 who had never been diagnosed with endometriosis, infertility, or cancer participated at the baseline in 1989. The results after the ten year study identified 1,130 nurses with laparoscopically confirmed endometriosis and no past infertility history. From that group, women with naturally red hair who had never been infertile had an increased rate (30%) of endometriosis; naturally red haired women who were infertile had a decreased rate of endometriosis. Regarding any link between the coagulation alterations, immune functions, and endometriosis, it was concluded the link was likely based on fertility.

In a smaller, private study undertaken by reproductive endocrinologists at a private university hospital, the object was to determine if infertile natural redheads had an increased prevalence of endometriosis. There were 143 infertile women in the study aged 23 to 41; 12 women had natural red hair. Ten of the 12 (83%) redheads were found to have endometriosis

Redheaded Oddities

compared to 55 of the 131 (42%) of the non redheads. The doctors concluded by statistical analysis, the 95% confidence intervals for the presence of endometriosis in infertile redheads was 55% to 100% versus 34% to 51% for non redheads. The results suggest an association between the occurrence of infertile women with natural red hair and the development of endometriosis. Hmmm, interesting.

This section was interesting research to me as a redhead who experienced these problems at an early age and thought all women had them. After reading hundreds of responses to my questions via social media from redheads also experiencing monthly hormonal/menstrual difficulties, I felt this needed to be addressed. Be reassured, you are not alone! Another curse redheads endure. Remember, we process pain differently.

As a teen I was practically incapacitated every month with severe cramps and heavy menstrual flows. My mother's helpful advice was "welcome to womanhood." After three pregnancies and one miscarriage, infertility did not seem to be my problem, but monthly hemorrhages were causing increased health difficulties. At the age of twenty-eight, I had a partial hysterectomy (uterus gone, ovaries left). The pathology report indicated severe endometriosis.

I am very familiar with the Nurses Health Study as I am one of the nurses studied in it and have been since it first began in 1976. The study will follow participating nurse's health histories until their death. My records were included in the study of endometriosis vs redheads as well as heart studies, stroke studies, gastrointestinal studies, breast health, diet, and some I am not even aware of. Questionnaires are sent to participants on a regular basis to update our current health status. Study results and conclusions are published when they become available.

Industrial Deafness

The term may also be referred to as noise induced hearing loss. Both are the gradual deterioration of hearing over a prolonged period of time due to repeated exposure to excessive noise. Studies have shown that hearing damage occurs with prolonged exposure to noise levels greater than 90 decibels. A lawn mower, a loud diesel truck, motorcycle, or loud food blender might operate at 90 decibels, but if you listen to any of

Redheaded Oddities

those for eight hours a day, five days a week, over several years, your hearing will eventually suffer.

Of course, loss of hearing also occurs normally with the aging process. Some loss may have occurred in early childhood with frequent ear infections resulting in one or more ruptured ear drum(s). Each rupture forms a scar on the drum which decreases the transmission of sound. Frequent ear infections in redheads, young and older, seem to be more prevalent than in other hair colors. Ringing in the ears, hissing, or buzzing (tinnitus) sounds are usually the first indications of potential hearing problems headed your way.

Most of us take advantage of the amazing job our ears do for us by not understanding the complexity of exactly what goes on beyond the outer ear. Deep inside the ear canal are the tiniest bones in our body working hard to allow us to hear and be able to communicate with the outside world.

As sound waves are captured by the outer ear and move down the ear canal (if it isn't clogged with wax) the waves bounce into the ear drum causing it to vibrate. The vibrations move on to the tiny bones (the malleus, incus, and stapes) in the middle ear which amplify the vibrations and send

Never Let A Ginger SNAP

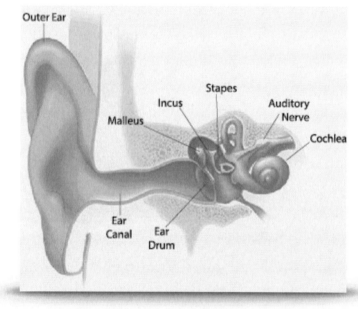

The outer and inner ear.

them to the <u>cochlea</u>. The cochlea looks like a tiny snail and is filled with fluid. It is within this snail shell all kinds of mysterious membranes, microscopic hair cells, and sensory cells break up the vibrations and send them to the appropriate channels to create an electrical signal. The auditory nerve picks up the signal and sends it to the brain which translates the sound for you: baby crying, smoke alarm sounding while cooking dinner, dog barking, ice cubes clinking in a glass, basketball bouncing off the roof… so that you can respond accordingly. Recall my story about screaming in

Redheaded Oddities

the operating room when I heard the pounding. My brain knew that pounding sound should hurt, so I responded to my brain's alarm system accordingly!

How are redheads more susceptible to hearing loss? Is that a fact or myth? Welllll, there are conflicting studies but the bottom line is, can you guess? MC1R.

One study, published in 2012, "Hair Color and Hearing Loss: A Survey in a Group of Military Men," was undertaken by the Iranian military to determine the susceptibility to noise-induced hearing loss in white soldiers with light colored hair vs black soldiers with dark colored hair. The study was to confirm or disprove the theory that low levels of pigmentation increase susceptibility to noise-induced hearing loss.

A total of fifty-seven military recruits participated. They were divided into two groups: light colored hair (blondes and light brown) and dark colored hair (dark brown and black). The testing noise levels were measured with varying levels of weapons fire, i.e. the number of rounds fired and the types of weapons used.

The small study and findings concluded that hair color could be used as an index for predicting susceptibility to noise-induced hearing loss in military environments. Those with light colored hair were much more susceptible to hearing loss compared to the dark haired soldiers.

Previous studies conducted by other researchers noted the effect of melanin on the susceptibility of hearing loss in persons with light colored eyes and hair vs darker eyes and hair. The military study did not specifically collect data on eye color, just hair color.

In 2017, the Nurse's Health Study published their results after investigating the role melanin plays in "Skin Pigmentation and Risk of Hearing Loss in Women." Approximately one-third of women in the United States suffer hearing loss by the age of 50; two-thirds by the age of 60. Hair color, skin tanning, and prolonged sun exposure were not associated with risk of hearing loss in white women. Black women are half as likely as whites to develop hearing loss, but the reasons for both were unclear. The study was undertaken to establish how and why. It would be much more in depth than the preceding military study.

A total of 49,323 white women were studied from 1982-2012 regarding their self-reported hearing loss, skin pigmentation, hair color, skin tanning ability, and prolonged sun exposure.

Redheaded Oddities

Further studies and data collection identified a correlation between skin melanocytes and inner ear melanocytes, specifically the cochlear melanocytes. Exciting news!

Melanocytes have antioxidant functions that might protect the inner ear from noise-induced hearing loss. Mutations in genes that result in deficient melanocytes result in impaired hearing. MC1R is the culprit again.

But wait, in the published study's conclusion, "characteristics associated with skin pigmentation were not associated with risk of hearing loss in white women, which suggests that differences in melanocytes may not be associated with risk of hearing loss in whites." (Translation: redheads do not have a susceptibility toward hearing loss.)

Hmmmm, confused? What do you think? Fact or myth? I think further studies are in order, but it sure seems to me that if we fair skinned, blue-eyed redheads have fewer melanocytes in our cochlea, we will be more likely to have hearing difficulties to begin with. Can you hear me NOW? WHAT?

*Redheads are not the type of women
you should put on speakerphone.*

Chapter 15
South Park - Gingervitis

"Gingervitis is real! Help find a cure".
Fear of redheads is gingerphobia.

South Park is an American animated sitcom which first aired on the Comedy Central television network August 13, 1997. The show features four eight-year-old boys and their misguided adventures in the small town of South Park, Colorado.

The boys are described on the show's website as:

Stan

Stan Marsh, the everyman of the bunch, the average American 4th grader.

Kyle Broflovski, the only Jewish boy, has a strong
Kyle
morality, often portrayed in his role satirically.

Eric

Eric Cartman, is loud, obnoxious, anti-Semitic, amoral, and antagonistic with a complete lack of morality.

Kenny McCormick, comes from a poor family, always
Kenny
wears his parka hood so tightly on his head, it covers his face and muffles his speech.

200

The show boasts it is the first weekly program to be rated TV-MA (Television - Mature Adult audiences). Various episodes have been described as raunchy and controversial. It also posts this fictitious disclaimer before each episode: "All characters and events in this show—even those based on real people—are entirely fictional. All celebrity voices are impersonated...poorly. The following program contains coarse language and due to its content it should not be viewed by anyone."

Over three hundred episodes have aired, but we will discuss the 136th episode which aired in the United States on November 9, 2005 titled "Ginger Kids." Here is a short synopsis of that episode:

On oral report day at school, Cartman delivers his class presentation titled: "Ginger kids: Children with Red Hair, Light Skin, and Freckles." He begins his report by calling people with red hair, freckles, and pale skin "gingers." He explains, gingers have a naturally occurring disease called "gingervitis." They are inhuman, have no souls, they are disgusting, can't live in sunlight, comparable to vampires, cursed by a gene... and must be rid from the earth to maintain the master race. He also terms hybrid redheads, those without pale skin or freckles, "daywalkers."

Kyle, who has red hair, speaks up against Cartman stating that red hair is an inheritable trait, not a disease. He tells Cartman he is going to cause trouble by stirring up hate, "Don't you understand what ignorant prejudice like that could lead to?" Cartman is not swayed and continues to instill prejudice towards redheaded kids at school and within the community.

Ginger abuse is real.

Kyle, Stan, and Kenny are upset about the prejudice which has gotten out of hand. One night while Cartman is sound asleep, the three sneak into his room with skin bleach, red hair dye, and Henna tattoos for dotting his face as freckles. Cartman freaks out when he wakes up and sees he has contracted the gingervitis disease. At school he is laughed at and cast out with the other gingers who must now eat their lunch in the hallway instead of the cafeteria. Cartman tries desperately to convince the school kids and the town's people he is the same as he was before contracting the disease. He establishes the "Ginger Separatist Movement" in an attempt to promote a more peaceful understanding of gingers. It doesn't work.

Gingers - Never trust them.

His movement becomes violent and Nazi-esque with protests and mayhem throughout the school and town, discriminating against anyone with red hair. The battle cry becomes, "The only way to fight hate…is with MORE hate!"

Gingers - One flaming hot minority.

At this point, the show was no longer entertaining to the vast majority of viewers, especially real redheads. Instead of being satirically funny it became hateful and racist. The writers/creators point was to show how easily people can be persuaded to hate other members of humankind without any justifying argument. Some say it missed the mark while others say it hit the mark on the (red) head. In either case, that show created a fire storm around the viewing world.

In 2008, three years after the *South Park* Ginger show, a fourteen-year old Canadian boy started a Facebook page titled, "Kick A Ginger" and established November 20, 2008, as Kick A Ginger Day. The page quickly accrued over five thousand "friends" who were encouraged to wreak violence upon redheads and to gear up: "Get them steel toes ready for our day."

In Canada, the U.S., and the U.K. reports flooded in to law enforcement and news agencies about young children being kicked, assaulted, bloodied, and fearing for their redheaded lives. This went on for several years on the appointed November 20th. In many cases, redheads were severely injured requiring hospitalization with younger children traumatized and fearful, just because they were redheads.

Very sadly, the suicide of a fourteen-year old boy and, later, a fifteen-year old girl were reported, both with red hair. Law enforcement labeled these incidents as hate crimes racially motivated even though the Canadian originator proclaimed it was all meant as a joke. A website, as opposed to the social media site for the group, was quickly established and declared, "Kick-a-ginger-day is not a serious event. It is a JOKE which originated from *South Park*. Don't kick anyone, we love gingers!" The website now sells T-shirts and redhead memorabilia.

Another Facebook page was created in 2009 as a counter to the Kick A Ginger Day: Kiss A Ginger Day! The date designated as Kiss A Ginger Day was January 20th. A disclaimer quickly appeared on the site: "Remember to make sure that the kissing is consensual for both parties, and perhaps avoid this holiday if you are sick or if you have any mouth infections." Then another special day began February 22: Hug A Ginger Day. There was likely a disclaimer to the hugging also!

In 2016, any further media/social site acknowledgement of Kick A Ginger Day was prohibited. The original Facebook site has been removed, but there are still a few negative sites that come up in a search. Many have failed to heed the ban and injuries to redheads on that day continue to be reported.

This author does not personally know any redhead that has not experienced bullying at a young age, even into adulthood. Bullying is one thing. Violence is another. Racial prejudice and discrimination completes the negative circle. None of these should be tolerated no matter what color your hair or skin is.

Either you like redheads or you are WRONG!

Chapter 16

International Redhead Days

*Redheads are a limited edition of fascination
with a unique and rare blend of awesomeness.*

That *South Park* television episode created a worldwide, redheaded uprising. A variety of social media pages and websites aimed at redheads began springing up; some mentioned earlier. Most of the sites were in support of redheads by countering the negative sites. Perhaps the most significant tribute to redheads began quite unknowingly in the Netherlands by an artist with BLONDE hair!

In 2005, Dutch painter Bart Rouwenhorst had an idea for an exhibit of fifteen paintings featuring dramatic portraits of redheaded women. He was intrigued by other artists who had painted masterpieces featuring women with red hair. Bart lived in the small city of Asten and had not personally seen many local redheads. He placed an advertisement in the local paper asking for fifteen volunteer natural redheads to model for portrait paintings. One hundred fifty quickly responded!

He was thrilled with the response and did not want to turn all of them away. He chose fourteen then organized a group photo shoot for the

International Redhead Days

Bart Rouwenhorst.

remaining redheads with a lottery for a chance at the fifteenth spot. He called this gathering Roodharigendag in Dutch, Redhead Day in English.

The first gatherings were for natural red haired women only while later events also included men with red hair. Even with the men included, the majority of attendees were women.

The second Roodharigendag Day was held on September 2, 2007 in the town of Breda with 800 redheads attending. Local school children were allowed the week off in preparation for the big event. The mayor opened the festivities by unveiling a beautiful painting of fifty redheads.

Realizing the increased interest of the event, several activities were included for the third Roodharigendag Day, held September 7, 2008. Forty-two activities were added with a multilingual program. Forty artists displayed their work. Press coverage was worldwide with articles about the event appearing in Norway, Hong Kong, and Chile. Two thousand redheads from fifteen

Never Let A Ginger SNAP

countries traveled to Breda to celebrate their unique hair color.

The 2009 event spread to two days. In 2011, it expanded again to three days. Every year thereafter the event seemed to explode with additional activities, photographers, artists, workshops, lectures, vendors, and musicians. The programs were printed in Dutch, English, and German.

In 2012, the event name was officially changed from Roodharigendag to Redhead Days. The event also drew record crowds of up to five thousand people from over sixty different countries. That year the Guinness Book of Records sent officials to record the gathering of the largest number of natural redheads standing together for ten minutes; 1,255. That record was broken in 2013 with 1,672 officially recorded. It was broken again in 2015 with 1,721.

In 2019, the event outgrew the original festival site and moved to Tilburg, the Netherlands. Bart Rouwenhorst continues as the organizer with hundreds of volunteers now assisting in staging the weeklong festival. Over 5,000 redheads and family members continue to attend from over 80 countries with a variety of media teams recording the festivities. There is no admission charge to this event and never has been. On the last afternoon of the festival, all natural redheads gather in a designated spot for a group photo. Photographers are hoisted high above the crowd in multiple locations to record the event both still photo and video. The festival continues to unite people from all over the world with its theme of celebrating individuality within one uniting factor - natural red hair.

As a result of the original Redheads Day event, similar events have been organized around the world: London, France, Italy, Germany, Canada, Ireland, Australia, Russia, Brazil, and multiple cities across the United States.

First held in June 2015, the Chicago suburb of Highwood boasts the largest Redhead Days festival in the United States. Portland, Oregon has a large festival, as well as New York, Georgia, and San Fransisco, California.

Although November 5 has been designated as International Redheads Day from the original event date, different cities and countries set their own "official" days. It can be confusing. Here are the names of a few U.S. events: World Redhead Day, Night of the Walking Redhead, National Love Your Red Hair Day.

Find a redhead event near you and attend! It could be a life altering awakening for you!

*What do you call six thousand redheads
gathered together?
A sunrise? A bonfire? A firestorm? A solar flare?
A love fest!*

September 2014 gathering at the Redhead Days
Breda, Netherlands.

Afterword

Redheads always have the last word.

Redheads are different! History has proved it, historians have documented it. Through the ages we have been mysterious outcasts accused, abused, tortured, drowned, burned at the stake. We have been deemed impatient, impulsive, rebellious, fighters, headstrong, reticent, suspicious, hostile, temperamental, stubborn, opinionated, quick tempered. Most recently we have been labeled as attractive, memorable, creative, unique, bold, independent, daring, adventurous, fearless, fiery, feisty, extravagant, idealistic, exceptional.

More and more folks worldwide are beginning to understand and accept that redheads are rare mutant novelties, unique, joyful, mirthful, fresh, radiant, and distinctive.

Redheads have become the unicorns of humans! We have been mythical creatures for centuries enthralling folks along the way. We are magical, mystical, enchanting, graceful, passionate, caring, nurturing, hopeful, and undoubtedly legendary. We are strong of character, powerful, confident, self-assured, empowered, and unstoppable. Like a unicorn, we can also become very dangerous when provoked.

Warning! Do not pet the redhead.
The unicorn could be a problem also.

Mark Twain conveyed to the world, "While the rest of the species is descended from apes, redheads are descended from cats." An interesting comparison! Like cats, we redheads are sleek, beautiful, intelligent, calculating, inquisitive, soft, fluffy, affectionate, lovable, playful, funny, entertaining, vocal, aloof, fastidious, loyal, sleepy, and sometimes, admittedly, lazy. We can be bossy and indifferent. Don't make us angry or we will hiss, bite, scratch, and poop in your shoes.

The author's beloved redhead.

Cats and redheads do what they want to do,
not what they are expected to do.

Afterword

Whether you relate best to the unicorn or the cat or a combination of the two, just remember to be the best you can be through good times and bad. We are confident, self-assured, and powerful, which makes us unstoppable! The non-reds/gingers depend on us to lead them.

*Remember, the scariest thing in the world
is a quiet, smiling redhead... looking at you.*

*Never upset a redhead -
it may be the last thing you ever do.*

*Let your red hair change the world
but don't let the world change your red hair.*

Definition of a redhead:
<u>R</u>are
<u>E</u>nchanting
<u>D</u>aring
<u>H</u>eadstrong
<u>E</u>mpowered
<u>A</u>dventurous
<u>D</u>efiant

"Ruadh gu brath" Gaelic for "Redheads Forever"

Acknowledgments

While on a long road trip last summer, the brilliant idea to write a book about redheads met with positive nods of approval from my two teen grandkids. They are both redheads with hair the same rusty red as mine used to be. I also have several redheaded friends who also encouraged the idea.

The mandated Covid virus quarantine forced me inside for more than three months so I commenced research, compiled notes, organized thoughts then pounded away on the computer and the idea became a reality.

I asked my redheaded family and friends to contribute their thoughts about growing up with the red curse. There was no arm twisting involved, they happily replied for which I am truly grateful! My long time friend, Mike, contributed his mother's no-nonsense comeback when he was constantly teased about being called a carrot top: "At least they're not calling you carrot butt." Mike served as one of my crewmen for our hot air balloon flights. Everyone thought he was my brother with the same rusty red hair color as mine; we nicknamed him Brother Mike. His red hair has

Acknowledgements

aged to snow white so he and his wife now serve as Santa and Mrs. Claus during the holidays.

Another adult, Jennifer, contributed her experiences with specific dental and surgical difficulties, namely pain control and anesthesia failures. She also replied, "Being a redhead definitely is a double-edged sword. Growing up, I wasn't teased, but I didn't embrace my MC1R gene until my adult years. I've learned that having red hair has its challenges, beyond looking physically different. Even though being a redhead can be a bit dramatic, I wouldn't change a thing!"

I was a bit surprised by the responses from the teen generation. The teasing and bullying doesn't seem to be as bad as it was for the older generation. Kady says she was never bullied and has always thought her beautiful red hair was a gift. She has studied the redhead history and loves the strong willpower and the fiery soul of our redheaded ancestors. "I couldn't ask for a better group to be a part of."

Morgan says she was teased a lot in her younger years which made her feel insecure. She has learned to love herself for who she is and now embraces being a redhead. "Just because I'm different doesn't mean it's bad; my hair is perfect the way it is. I don't need to be the same as everyone else to be pretty or good enough."

Brady says, "I honestly love all that comes with having red hair. There are very few people that have it, and I am lucky to be one of them!"

A big thank you to all those redhead social media "friends" who weighed in with their experiences, problems, and ideas. You all fueled the research necessary to find answers, prove facts and dispel myths.

As always, I must thank my supportive husband and computer geek, Ernie Hagen. He is beginning to understand my freak-outs when the computer hisses at me: he fixes me a Dr. Pepper, tells me to calm down, and takes care of the computer problem.

Thanks to my faithful editor, Julie Cline, who has survived another book assignment. Hopefully, this one was more fun than WWII history.

Cover designs and layout assistance from Marty Bicek have always been appreciated, but even more so with this book. The cover photograph is his daughter, my granddaughter, Morgan.

Bibliography

Articles

Banks, Sandy. " 'Kick a Ginger Day' leaves a bitter lesson." *Los Angeles Times*. December 5, 2009.

Baylor college of Medicine. "The Myth Behind Adrenal Fatigue." March 16, 2018.

Brown, Herman, B.S.; Klauder, Joseph, M.D. "Sulphur Content of Hair and of Nails in AB- Normal States." *JAMA*. April 1933.

"Do Mosquitoes Like Some People More Than Others?" *HuffPost*. June 5, 2013.

Faragher, Aliza Kelly. "How to Tap Into Your Own Psychic Abilities." *Allure*. July 2, 2018.

Gillan, Audrey. "Ginger gene makes redheads more sensitive to the cold." September 11, 2005.

Kris. "Difference between being an empath and being a psychic medium." *Your Empath Destiny*. March 30, 2017.

Lin, Brian M. et al."Skin Pigmentation and Risk of Hearing Loss in Women." *American Journal of Epidemiology*. May 19, 2017.

March, Bridget. "13 Amazing Facts About Redheads That Everyone Needs To Know." *Cosmopolitan*. April 5, 2017.

Melnick, Meredith. "Why Surgeons Dread Redheads." *Time*. December 10, 2010.

Bibliography

Miller, Danae. "The Physiology of Psychic People and Psychic Ability." *The Weiler Psi*. May 10, 2018.

Newman, Tim. "Is Adrenal Fatigue A Real condition?" *Medical News Today*. June 27, 2018.

Osterloff, Emily. "What is Ambergris?" Natural History Museum.

Otorhinolaryngol, Iran J. "Hair Color and Hearing Loss: A Survey in a Group of Military Men." Iranian Journal of Otorhinolaryngology. April 3, 2012.

Parker-Pope, Tara. "The Pain of Being a Redhead." *The New York Times*. August 6, 2009.

Parry, Hannah. "Red-headed school kids targeted by other students on 'Kick a Ginger Day' inspired by South Park." *Daily Mail*. November 26, 2015.

Riddle, Sharla. "How Bees See And Why It Matters." *Bee Culture*. May 20, 2016.

Robbins, Tom. "Ode To Redheads." *GQ*. June 1988.

Sessler, Daniel, M.D.; Liem, Edwin B. M.D. et al. "Increased Sensitivity to Thermal Pain and Reduced Subcutaneous Lidocaine Efficacy in Redheads." *Anesthesiology*. March 2005.

Sessler, Daniel, M.D.; Liem, Edwin B. M.D. et al. "Anesthetic Requirement is Increased in Redheads." *Anesthesiology*. August 2004.

"Science Confirms Redheads Are Equipped With Some Weird Genetic Superpowers." *GQ*. March 12, 2019.

Bibliography

Smithfield, Brad. "Howdy Doody: The Most Celebrated Children's Show in Television History." *The Vintage News*. May 18, 2017.

Vittek, Shelly. "Redhead Days International Festival." National Geographic.

Walker, Peter. "Police Called in to School Over 'Kick A Ginger Kid Day'." *The Guardian*. October 18, 2013.

"We Should All Know These 7 Things About Our Blood Type!" *NJABP*. August 18, 2017.

Williams, Megan Mansell. "Secrets of Redheads." *Discover Magazine*. November 21, 2005.

Books

Douglas, Stephan. *The Redhead Encyclopedia.* Stonecastle Literary Group. March 1996.

Harvey, Jacky Collisss. *Red - A History of The Redhead*. The Black Dog & Leventhal Publishers. June 2015.

LaRosa, Erin. *Inside The Secret Society of Red Hair. The Big Redhead Book*. St. Martin's Press. August 2017.

Vendetti, Adrienne & Stephanie. *How To Be A Redhead*. Page Street Publishing. April 2016.

Bibliography

Ginger Parrot.co.uk

(Note: The following titles were all utilized as research material from the above website.)

"Are Redheads at Higher Risk of Disease?"

"Are Redheads More Likely To Be Left-Handed?"

"Calendar of Redhead Events 2020."

"Cute and Creative Nicknames for Redheads."

"Do Redheads Bruise More Easily Than Other Hair Colors?"

"Do Redheads Smell Different?"

"Facts and Myths About Red Hair."

"How the MC1R 'ginger gene' was discovered."

"How Redheads' Vitamin D powers Can Protect Them Against Seasonal Affective Disorder (SAD)."

"MC1R Ginger Gene Linked to Parkinson's Disease and Melanoma Risk."

"Redheads and Achromotrichia: Do Gingers Go Grey?"

"Redheads and Anesthesia: Fact or Myth?"

"Should Redheads Take Vitamin D Supplements?"

"The History of Redheads and Witchcraft."

"The Ancient History of Redheads and Ginger Hair."

"The Debate of Redheads and Anesthesia."

"The Importance of Sun Hat Protection for Redheads."

"What Does 'Bluey' Mean?"
"What Does 'Carrot Top' Mean?"
"What Does 'Duracell' Mean?"
"What Does 'Firecracker' Mean?"
"What Does 'Fire Crotch' Mean?"
"What Does 'Ginger Nut' Mean?"
"What Does Gingervitis Mean?"
"What Does 'Matchstick' Mean?"
"What Does 'Rusty' Mean?"
"Where Does The Term 'Ginger' Come From?"
"Will I have Ginger Babies?"

Social Media Sites
(Note: The following Social Media sites were helpful to the author in obtaining thoughts, questions and views from site members.)

Beautiful Redheads.
Blue-eyed Redheads.
Ginger Nation.
How to be a Redhead.
Just For Redheads.
Natural Redheads Only.
Real Redheads Only.
Redhead Secret Club.
The Beauty of Redheads.
The Redhead Community.

Bibliography

Websites/Webpages

"7 Best Metals or Material for Sensitive Ears." afashionblog.com/best-metals-for-sensitive-ears/

"10 Famous Myths About Redheads Debunked." howtobearedhead.com

"39 Redhead Facts Too Crazy to Believe." factretriever.com/redhead-facts

Adkins, Jen. "UVA and UVB Rays: The Difference." March 2, 2020. bride.com/uva-and-uvb-rays-3013648

Benjamin, Kerry. "Why Protecting Your Acid Mantle is So Important." //stackedskincare.com/blogs/blog/why-protecting-your-

Binns, Corey. "The Shocking Truth Behind Electricity." April 17, 2006. livescience.com/4077-shocking-truth-static-electricity

"Birthmarks." //medlineplus.gov/birthmarks.html

Buka, Bobby Dr. "How to tell the difference between a mole and a freckle." the dermspecs.com/blog/

Burns, Angie."Redhead Pain." March7, 2012. sunstoneonline.com/redhead-pain-sensitivity/

Chearuil, Emma Ni. " Historical Facts about Redheads and Witchcraft." October 23, 2017. howtobearedhead.com

Cherry, Kendra. "Color Psychology: Does it Affect How You Feel?" July 17, 2019. verywellmind.com/color-psychology.

Cherry, Kendra. "The Color Psychology of Red." January 8, 2020. verywellmind.com

Bibliography

"Danger." June 2015. fifthwense.org.uk/danger

Davis, Jeanie Lerche. "Redheads Need More Anesthesia." October15, 2002. webmd.com/women/news

DeNoon, Daniel J. "Surgery Riskier for Redheads? Evidence Slim." December 9, 2010. webmd.com/pain-management/news

"Fact or Fiction: Do Redheads Feel More Pain?" October25, 2017. pbs.org/newshour/science/

"Facts About Endometriosis." endometriosis.org

Felson, Sabrina M.D. "Adrenal Fatigue: Is it Real?" February 8, 2019. webmd.com/a-z-guides/adrenal-

Gill, Karen, Richardson, M.D. "How Common Are People with Red Hair and Blue Eyes?" September 18, 2018. health line.com/health/red-hair

Heubeck, Elizabeth. "Are You A Mosquito Magnet?" January 31, 2012. webmd.com/allergies/features/are-you-mosquito-

"How Do We Hear?" May 2015. midcd.nih.gov/health/how-do-we-hear

Jaliman, Debra M.D. "Sunburn." July 16, 2018. webmd.com/skin-problems-and-treatments/guide/ s

Kraft, Sy."How to treat and prevent sunburn." June 26, 2017. medicalnewstoday.com/articles

LaFuente, Cat. "Myths about redheads you always thought were true." April 16, 2019. thelist.com/15050/myths-about-redheads-you-

LaVelle, Naomi. "How and why do we get freckles?" irishexaminer.com/lifestyle/features

Bibliography

Lefler, Leah. "Blood Types: History, Genetics, and Percentages Around The World." November 14, 2018. ow/cation.com/stem/blood

Mayo Clinic Staff. "Nickel Allergy." May 10, 2019. mayoclinic.org/diseases-conditions/nickel-allergy/

Mayo Clinic Staff. "Stress Management. March 19, 2019. mayoclinic.org/healthy-lifestyle/stress-management

Mayo Clinic Staff. "Sunburn. Diagnosis and Treatment." medicalnewstoday.com/articles/176441#sunburn/

Miller, Tom."Redheads Have More Sex According to Survey." August 6, 2007. yourtango.com/20071275/redheads-have-more-sex

Missmer, Stacey A."Natural Hair Color and the Incidence of Endometriosis." March 9, 2006. //pubmed.ncbi.nim.nih.gov/16580366/

Missmer, Stacey A, et al. "Red Hair Gene Not Linked to Endometriosis. June 2006. //endometriosis.org/news/research/red-hair-gene-not-linked-to-endometriosis

"National Kick A Ginger Day." November 26, 2008. //hoaxes.org/weblog/comments

Peirson, Erica M.D. "Genetics of Red Hair." September 21, 2016. peirsoncenter.com/articles/

"People with Black Skin Better Protected Against Hearing Loss. October 11, 2011. hear-it-org/people-with-black-skin-better-ptotected

Ratini, Melinda DO. "What is Melanin?"July 10, 2019. webmd.com/a-to-z-guides/what-is-melanin?

Bibliography

"Reasons Sex with Redheads is Simply the Best, According to Science."
sheknows.com/health-and-wellness/articles

Redfire67. "Redheads Have Magical Powers."
May 18, 2018. redhairedroots.com/tag/psychic/

"Redhead Days - Fact or Fiction."
redheaddays.nl/en/about/everything-about-red-hair/

"Redheads do feel more pain - and they're tougher then anyone else."2009-2017.
zmescience.com/science/redheads-feel-more-pain

"Redheads Have Greater Fear of Dentists."
August 1, 2009.
OR.org/news/redorbit-redheads-2009-08-01.html

Sager, Jeanne. "Endometriosis Symptons: What's Really Going On Down There?" March 7, 2018.
Healthyway.com

Sheldon, Natasha. "The Unexpectedly Violent History of Red Hair."
history collection.co/unexpectedly-violent-history

Solo, Andre. "13 Signs That You're an Empath."
January 18, 2019.
highlysensitiverefuge.com/empath-signs

South Park Studios. "Ginger Kids (Episode).
//wiki.southpark.cc.com/wiki/ginger_kids_(episode)

Spencers Solicitors. "Industrial Deafness Guide."
spencersolicitors.com/accident-guides/industrial

Starbuck, Jamison Dr. "Freckles, Moles, and Birthmarks: Dr. Starbuck explains." August 2018.
mtpr.org/post/freckles-moles-and-birthmarks-

Bibliography

Stevenson, John. "What is a Lightning Rod and How Does it Work?" July 7, 2017.
electricianmurrieta.net/lightening-rod/

"Strange Facts About Redheads You Never Knew Before."
rd.com/culture/facts-about-readheads/

"Vitamin D deficiency." healthline.com/nutrition/

"What Causes Freckles?" wonderopolis.org/wonder/

"What Do Unicorns Represent? Symbolism and Mythology." Unicorn Yard.
//unicornyar.com/what-do-unicorns-represent/

"What is National Redhead Day?"
national today.com/national-redhead-day

"What is the Acid Mantle and How Does Toning Help Maintain It?" cocokind.com/blogs/news/

"What is the difference between Psychic Ability and Intuition?" keen.com/articles/psychic/

"Why do honeybees die after they sting you?" June 23, 2011.
//earthsky.org/earth/why-do-bees-die-after-they-sting-you

"Why is smell important?" March 19, 2012.
air-aroma.com/blog/why-is-smell-important

"Why Kiss A Ginger Day Was Invented."
howtobearedhead.com/why-kiss-a-ginger-day-was-invented

"Why Your Skin Turns Green After Wearing Rings And How to Prevent it."
spoonuniversity.com/healthier/skin-turns-green

Bibliography

Woodworth, Steven H. M.D. "A prospective study on the association between red hair color and endometriosis in fertile patients." science direct.com/science/article/abs/pii

Wikipedia

(Note: The topics listed below were the author's search subjects. Links to their original sources were previously listed if utilized. Dates searched are listed along with the military time of search.)

Bee Sting. June 11, 2020. 1330.

Bozo The Clown. March 28, 2020. 1244.

Cherry Ames. February 21, 2020. 0920.

Cholecalciferol. April 27, 2020.

Cochlea. July 4, 2020.1354.

Freckle. April 19, 2020. 1443,

Ginger Kids. June 6, 2020. 1023.

Gloria Winters. March 26, 2020. 1357.

Hemangioma. July 9, 2020. 1335.

How to be a redhead. June 17, 2020. 1435.

Howdy Doody. February 20, 2020. 1143.

Human Skin. April 27, 2020. 1514.

Kenneth Arnold UFO Sighting. March 28, 2020. 1517.

Melanin. April 24, 2020. 1451.

Psychic. April 16, 2020. 1403.

Red Hair. April 18, 2020. 1218.

Redhead Day. June 6, 2020. 1122.

Bibliography

Sky King. February 20, 2020. 1300.

South Park. June 6, 2020. 1033.

Sunburn. April 30, 2020. 1014.

The Mickey Mouse Club. February 20, 2020. 1253.

The Shari Lewis Show. February 20, 2020. 1228.

Vitamin D. April 27, 2020. 1215.

Watch Mr. Wizard. February 20, 2020. 1237.

Willard Scott. March 28, 2020. 1315.

About the Author

Author Claudia Hagen has published several non-fiction books featuring women during WWII, as well as two memoirs and two children's books. Visit her website for a list of titles. All her books have their own public Facebook page under  each of the titles. Most of her books are available for order on Amazon.com.

After forty-one years as a registered nurse and twelve years as a commercially rated hot air balloon pilot, Claudia is now retired and living in California's Central Valley. When not researching and writing, she enjoys reading, gardening, and trying to stay out of trouble. She is a typical redhead. Even though her rusty locks have now transitioned to white, the redhead personality traits remain. Beware!

Visit her website to learn more about her books:
www.claudiahagen.com

Made in United States
North Haven, CT
16 January 2022